Open-Eyed Adoption

Praise for Open-Eyed Adoption

Read *Open-Eyed Adoption* to learn you're not alone in the unforeseen, surprising, and difficult realities of adoption. As Robin takes you on her vulnerable journey as an adoptive mother with humility and courage, she will introduce you to fellow travelers, and together, you will find companionship, understanding, support, resources, and hope for your own journey.

Nancy Schornack, LMHC, CDWC

What I wouldn't give to have been able to read this book before we adopted our two children! Robin Hitt does an exceptional job of educating adoptive parents from every angle. Her book, *Open-Eyed Adoption*, shares wisdom from her own experience raising adopted children as well as personal testimonies from other adoptive parents. Robin also explains the research and science behind an adoptee's way of processing feelings and emotions and provides avenues to understanding and interpreting the adoptee's unique way of viewing relationships. I am excited to apply what I have learned to my relationships with my teenage daughters. *Open-Eyed Adoption* is a MUST READ for anyone who has adopted children or is considering adoption.

Michelle Dutton, adoptive mom of two beautiful bi-racial girls

Robin Hitt has voiced, researched, and answered the questions many adoptive families struggle over with rich interviews and anecdotes. *Open-Eyed Adoption* is a must-read for adoptive parents, grandparents, and adoptees.

Sarah Latchaw, author, adoptive and foster mother

I especially enjoyed reading the stories from the adopted children. Their perspectives were very helpful.

CW, adoptive mom

Open-Eyed Adoption was a balm to my soul!

SL, adoptive mom

Reading *Open-Eyed Adoption* has been like peeling an onion . . . lots of flavor brought on tears, but the delicious result was worth it!

JH, adoptive mom

Robin has a very good handle on the big picture and the need for better education on the process and expectations.

CH, adoptive mom

Open-Eyed Adoption has been a game-changer for me. I am an adoptive mom and knowing now what I wish I had known then is eye-opening. Thank you, Robin, for your labor of love!

GW, adoptive mom

As an adult adoptee I love that *Open-Eyed Adoption* speaks with such tenderness regarding what adoption can bring to a family while still being clear about the reality of how incredibly complex adoption is. I found *Open-Eyed Adoption* to be a loving tribute of a mother's love and a gift to those who desire to seek education and awareness on how to best support themselves and the adoptee in their life.

Erica E., adoptee

OPEN EYED ADOPTION

Real Help for Those Parenting Adoptees

ROBIN HITT

NEW YORK

LONDON • NASHVILLE • MELBOURNE • VANCOUVER

OPEN-*EYED* ADOPTION

Real Help for those Parenting Adoptees

Published in New York, New York, by Morgan James Publishing. Morgan James is a trademark of Morgan James, LLC. www.MorganJamesPublishing.com

Proudly distributed by Ingram Publisher Services.

ISBN 9781631959806 paperback
ISBN 9781631959813 ebook
Library of Congress Control Number:
2022938856

Cover Design by:
Christopher Kirk
www.GFSstudio.com

Interior Design by:
Chris Treccani
www.3dogcreative.net

Morgan James is a proud partner of Habitat for Humanity Peninsula and Greater Williamsburg. Partners in building since 2006.

Get involved today! Visit MorganJamesPublishing.com/giving-back

In memory of my Donnas:
Donna Maree, who gave me life and a lifetime
of unconditional love.

Donna Kay, who always believed in me, called me out,
and pushed me to write this book.

I am standing on your shoulders. I will never forget.
I feel you even now.

Table of Contents

Introduction

The visceral stab in my heart gripped me and wouldn't let go. I felt as though I couldn't breathe. I had to get away from everyone, so I retreated to our car in the garage. Our happy-ever-after adoption story was crumbling before my eyes. These beautiful children had gone "off-script." The fairytale was over, and something had to change.

What had happened to my beautiful adoption story? We are all a byproduct of nature *and* nurture. Our adoption agency told us that 90 percent of a child's outcome is based on nurture: parenting and environment. We believed them. Now, most studies reveal the impact falls somewhere between 35 and 50 percent nature and 40–60 percent nurture, with "experiences" rounding out the whole. So where did we go wrong? What was once our idyllic family had become a convoluted ball of yarn—one that would start me on a journey of discovery. This discovery would lead me to realize that adoption, with all its moving parts, is a lifelong deer path toward understanding. I'm imagining a trail of breadcrumbs left along an isolated trail for the trekker to find their way home.

There's much to discover in the adoption *triad*. I learned that adoption always involves a birth mother, an adoptee, and an adoptive parent(s). These three entities are inextricably tied together for life. For an adoption to take place, there is usually someone who feels they are losing and someone who feels they are gaining. The intricacies of the invisible connection continue far beyond the eighteen years it takes to raise children to adulthood. Most of the awareness that takes place comes in spurts and halted moments, followed by a flow of painful realities until we become equipped.

Adoptive parents are an army. Currently, there are roughly 100 million Americans who have adoption in their immediate family, whether this includes adopting, placing, or being adopted. An army needs to be equipped. If you are considering adoption, have adopted and are currently raising your children, or are a foster parent, this book is for you. I dare say the contents spelled out here will also help adoptive parents whose children have left the nest. Adult adoptees and therapists may find help in these pages too. Within *Open-Eyed Adoption*, you will hear from adoptive parents, doctors, therapists, birth mothers, and adult adoptees, as I summarize my interviews and present the distilled culmination of these brave and helpful souls' stories below.

I believe every one of us shares a common humanity. We all have flaws and things that plague us. You could say we're all broken in some way. We get broken as we live. Brokenness happens over time through various circumstances, as others hurt us in big and small ways. We've been betrayed. We've believed lies. We've lived through trauma and experienced things we never wanted. Even if we had a stellar family of origin, we received messages from society that have shaped us. In this light, we're all in need of healing. It's important to highlight that members of the adoption triad have unique challenges that biological children and families do not have to manage. This is an important distinction. The issues of the adopted heart are not worse than the biological framework; they're just different.

I wrote *Open-Eyed Adoption* to pry the gates of knowledge and understanding wide open. In searching for answers to the challenges I faced while raising our adopted daughters, I noticed a severe lack of information on the bookshelves. I vacillated between telling myself, "All is normal" and "Something is wrong here, but I have no idea what I'm looking at right now." Justifying my questions, I thought raising teens is always a challenge, so I pressed on in silence without adequate support for the things I was experiencing.

Meanwhile, our teens were soldiering on in their own silent ways. Without resources or the slightest understanding of why they felt as they did, they were left in the dark with only their feelings. Many times, this resulted in them feeling out of step with their peers, knowing their situation was different, but trying to live as though it wasn't.

In addition, those who made the difficult and loving choice to place their children for adoption have also had to grapple with feelings of isolation, regret, and all the "what ifs." These questions can be hidden in each segment of their journey, beginning with the date they created life to the day they signed the papers for the adoption to become finalized. But it doesn't stop there. Their life journey will forever be tied to this reality.

I can tell you that, as an adoptive mom, there is sheer joy in receiving a little life into your heart and home. All the expectations and excitement that swirl around the adoptive parent is hard to contain. I know, for me, I felt as if my heart might burst.

That said, there was another woman across town whose heart was near bursting for an entirely different reason. That woman would gain certain freedom over time, but her heart would never be free of the invisible cord that connected her with the child. Nowadays, science tells us there is an exchange of cellular activity while pregnant, an exchange that happens between a pregnant woman and the child she carries. It's a lifelong bond, no matter if the woman raises the child or not.

Adult adoptees have reported to me all sorts of emotionally charged feelings. Some acted "good" so they wouldn't be sent back. Some tested every boundary to see how deeply they were loved by their adoptive parents. Still others were oblivious to their invisible needs until a certain age or when they met their birth families. Every person interviewed for this book has a story.

You will hear my story, which takes you from the sublime to bewilderment and into better clarity. As the book unfolds, I will bring you along to more understanding of what the adoptee and parent are experiencing. Gaining perspective on each member of the adoption triad, you will receive an education and resources. You'll get a front-row seat in the interviews of adoptive family members who are being brutally honest as well as how each person's faith plays into the process. Therapists and doctors lend their expertise in treating the adoptees' challenges, be it physical or emotional, including strategies to manage reactive attachment disorder (RAD).

You will learn the importance of building your adoptive community, how to unpack your child's personality, and how to better communicate with your child. Adult adoptees generously shed light on their thoughts and have opened a door for a better understanding of their ways of thinking. For clarification, I've referred to those who have adopted as adoptive parents. Those who have been adopted, I'm calling adoptees. I realize that adoption is something that happens in one's life and does not define one's identity. It's much like referring to those who have cancer as cancer patients or those who were born in the years 1997–2012 as Gen Z. This is something that has happened or that groups them with others who have had like occurrences. I do want to say here that all of the parents' and adoptees' names have been changed to protect their identities. That said, their stories are true.

Since there is such a great need for a hug, I've included a chapter on self-compassion. Detangling the myth that self-care is selfish, you will be permitted to take a breath and learn to love yourself while in the middle of making mistakes.

Does this all sound good? Well, strap on your seatbelt, and let's take a ride.

Chapter One

SUCKER-PUNCHED PARENTING

One cold December night, my husband Jon and I took our two young adult daughters to the movies to focus on something bright. As a family, we were emerging from a tough season and seeking entertainment to bring us together. While waiting to enter the theater, our daughter blurted out, "Hey, my birth mom just tried to get hold of me on Facebook. I'm not sure what I'm going to do yet, but that was neat."

In moments, I felt my heart race, and I was barely conscious of the fact I was holding my breath. Why now? Would I ever have our daughters' whole hearts? Why does adoption always have to be in the background? This one announcement sent me into such a quick downward spiral, I thought I may never recover. She had just been through an emotional breakup with someone who had been divisive to our family. While we were relieved that this relationship had ended, tensions with our daughter remained. I wasn't ready to tackle anything else. It scared me that, in one moment, it seemed as if everything I'd invested in her could just disappear. I could be rendered useless and forgotten. In her excitement and curiosity, she was unaware of how these words affected my heart. I felt threatened, but I remained silent. As the theater went dark and the movie began, I saw the characters on the big screen moving their mouths but heard nothing. To this day, I couldn't tell you one thing about that movie. I simply sat there, feeling sad, vulnerable, and worthless for nearly two hours.

This daughter had never expressed an interest in meeting her birth mom before. All I've sacrificed . . . all I believed would happen. Throughout the movie, my brain was trying to process this new place. The story I told myself in those long minutes was this: "She will leave us and cling to her birth mom. She will find joy there and never want to come and spend time with us. Why would she? We've imposed our beliefs, our values, and our family culture. She will find absolute freedom there. A different family culture. She will forget me." The surge of adrenaline was unstoppable. At the same time, I was planted in my theatre chair like I'd been riveted there by a substantial force. The movie played on. The tornadic storm of failure and loss swirled around my mind with such intensity, I thought it could surely be heard over the entertainment speakers. In those moments, the culmination of the last twenty-two years had all caught up with me and landed with a thud, right on my heart. The weight was unbearable.

When the movie ended, we got into the car, and excited chatter over the plot filled the air. But my head was filled with all the emotions that came with her brief announcement in the lobby. Once home, each entered the house and continued into their own spaces. Still gripped with emotion, I went back to the car in the garage. In that privacy, I wept from somewhere deep in my gut. I cried until my head hurt. And then, in a moment of clarity, I wondered if I was the only adoptive parent that felt like such a failure. After years of telling her I loved her, rocking her to sleep at night, calming her fears, and being present through her times of difficulty, how could I have not gained her complete loyalty and love? Could there be answers out there somewhere for me?

I remembered a couple who had adopted a child the same day we did. I thought of their names and wondered if maybe they would talk to me. I called the adoption agency and asked them to give this couple my name and number in hopes they would call me. While I waited, I imagined that their family was perfect. I told myself I would just humble myself and learn something from the mom if she called. I braced myself for humiliation at the way I'd parented, considering how *she* had probably parented. My thoughts ran away with themselves and then the phone rang.

Susan and Jeff are a beautiful couple, and they had adopted multiple children through the same agency we had used. Susan's voice was gentle, and she seemed genuinely happy to hear from me. We planned to talk later. She assured me she had much to say on the subject. Well, this pacified me for the time. I was intrigued and nervous, but I was excited to be getting to talk with another adoptive mom. I'd never done that. I didn't know I needed to.

We discovered we lived in the same area, so we made plans for lunch in the not-too-distant future. I felt grateful for any insights she would share with me. Obviously, I had a lot to learn.

To my shock, Susan had been through much pain of her own. Her story unfolded in paragraphs about her kids and the suffering she and Jeff had endured. Like us, they gave and gave to their kids. They, too, didn't understand the patterns of behavior in their children that had emerged. Behaviors included self-sabotage, poor relationships, lack of self-worth, and absence of a vision for their lives . . . you get the idea. Their kids found it difficult to fit in.

Some acted out in reckless ways and were promiscuous and daring. Some were quiet, introverted, and lacking in confidence. A common theme was that they were living beneath their capabilities.

Susan described the kind of upbringing they afforded their kids. They had them in weekly church services, camps, private schools, and playdates with friends—all the "good stuff." They were vigilant parents and worked hard to ensure their children knew they were loved. Despite their best efforts, each of their children had issues related to their adoption that showed up over time. Some had met their birth moms. Some had not. It had been a bumpy ride, even right up to our lunch conversation.

I jotted down notes as we talked. At the close of our two-hour lunch, we decided there was much more we needed from each other. We agreed to meet monthly for a while. I saw there was more to this adoption "process" than I ever thought. As themes emerged and our collective pain continued, I knew I had to share what I was learning with other adoptive parents. And that research is what you're now holding in your hands.

This is not an exhaustive resource, by any means. For this book, which is to encourage adoptive parents, I will not linger over any one category of challenges that adoptees and their parents experience. Each category presents another layer of developmental hurdles that need to be understood and addressed.

For instance, adopting a child who is biracial, has special needs, or is addicted to drugs or alcohol will come with an extra set of needs that other adoptees might not have. Adopting an older child who has already experienced difficult events will present additional needs. These children will have to work through the psychological, and sometimes even the physical, pain they've endured. This is often referred to as developmental trauma— occurring either in the womb or after birth. Adoption, under the

best circumstances, adds a developmental layer to each milestone and task of childhood.

Open-Eyed Adoption is an attempt to share my pain and the pain of others to let the adoptive parent know they are not alone. Hopefully, you will better understand what you're seeing and experiencing. At the end, I've listed additional resources to lead you to further information.

While I cannot endorse or recommend certain treatments because I've not tried all of them, I hope to give you every tool that's reported to have helped one of the adoptive parents I've interviewed or that I have learned has helped others through my research. Perhaps these tools can light your way when it's dark. And just like this book has a beginning, a middle, and an end, so do our lives. We must continue to the end to discover the result. With greater understanding, hopefully, the best is yet to come.

Chapter Two

STARRY-EYED IN TEXAS

She had me at the door. There she was, a new human being, complete with a head full of dark brown hair that stood up every which way, reddened skin, and arms and legs still unfolding from the fetal position she had been in for the last nine months in utero. I couldn't believe this moment had come. They were actually going to place this perfect child in our arms for us to take home and raise as our daughter. Tiny worries nettled my brain. What if we mess it up? What if we don't know "stuff?" Will we be enough? Why had I not gotten a degree in parenting instead of nursing?

As I approached this tiny baby dressed in pink and wrapped in a homemade patchwork quilt, my questions fled my mind because I was awestruck at the sheer magic of this exquisite space. It was as if time stood still for those moments. After welcoming us, the caseworker from the adoption agency smiled and gently placed her in my arms. I was speechless. She was so beautiful. So perfect. Such an answer to prayer. It was all just so surreal.

I had been working in the intensive care unit (ICU) and other areas within local hospitals as a registered nurse (RN) and had taken care of hundreds of patients with all sorts of conditions over the last eight years, but suddenly, this mattered so much more than any of that. Her weight felt heavy in my arms and somehow her total dependency on us made all the other ICU experiences pale in comparison. Briefly, those haunting questions returned. What are we supposed to do with her? What's the *right* thing? I didn't want to miss any of this.

But there was no checklist, no regimen like I was used to at the hospital, where everything was spelled out by either the doctor or a policy and procedure manual. No. Being of sound mind and reasonable intelligence, we were just supposed to know what to do with this baby.

I just held her. And stared at her. I watched every twitch, every movement, and was spellbound. When she stirred in my arms, the agent offered me a bottle, saying it was time for her feeding. I wondered if she'd take it and how long to leave it there. She willingly took the milk offered, and I felt accomplished. After I'd had my turn holding her, I turned to Jon, who waited patiently beside me, and asked him if he'd like to hold her. He took her gently, and we both smiled at the thought of us three becoming a family. He, there in his pink ball cap in honor of this occasion, me in my blue and red sundress, and this precious new soul we were holding. We would be referred to from now on as the Jon Hitt Family.

Fourteen years earlier, Jon and I married at age twenty and put off having a family for three to four years to have some time together before our attentions were divided. When we decided it was time to begin our family four years into our marriage, we learned that becoming pregnant wasn't as easy as we'd thought. The next ten years would prove arduous, painful, and shaming. Though we both had careers that kept us busy—me in nursing and Jon in aviation—there was always an ache deep inside. As I attended all of my friends' children's births, went to many baby showers, and remained seated on Mother's Day when the pastor asked the mothers to stand, it all wore wear on me in ways I found debilitating at times. Another pressing fact to deal with was all the "unwanted babies" around me. There were the unplanned pregnancies among a couple of teenagers, the career women who never wanted children, and the cases of aborted[1] and abused children I knew were out there. Why was it so easy for these women to conceive yet impossible for me? I asked God *why* all the time but never got a satisfactory answer. So I just kept living and working and interacting with good friends, and tolerated the platitudes and "reasons" people gave for our infertility, which were unsolicited, of course. We had endured fertility testing, artificial insemination, and difficult protocols prescribed by the fertility specialist. One day, our doctor pointedly told us that 3 percent of the nation's infertility cases were diagnosed as "unexplainable," and we fell into that category. Then, we went home.

The word *adoption* came up, but I wouldn't hear of it. Jon and I had been childhood sweethearts and in love for many years, and I desperately wanted to carry *his* child. Hope was now only a glimmer, but I still didn't want to consider adoption and give up on having biological children. When Jon asked me about it, I said, "Give me one more year, and if nothing happens, I'll talk about it." He, very literally, marked it down in his calendar. One year

---

1   *If you are suffering from the aftermath of having had an abortion, please reach out to support and recovery groups. Search "Abortion Recovery" for someone near you.

later, to the day, he asked me again. I melted into a puddle of tears and failure. I was at the end of myself.

Some time went by, and my heart softened enough to be willing to talk with a nearby agency we'd had some dealings with years earlier through a friend. The conversation was overwhelming, with a lot of statistics on why people should adopt. It left me wanting to run from the whole idea. I felt very much like I wouldn't be a good person if I didn't pursue this because there were so many children who needed homes and families. I resented being made to feel guilty about something so personal. Adoption remained out of the question.

A few more months passed, and I flew to the Dominican Republic to board a medical missions ship where I assisted in surgeries aimed to uncross eyes, repair cleft lips, correct cleft palates, and treat children for burns. While there, I had an experience that turned me on my heels. There were many activities the medical helpers could engage in, such as workshops, checking out local coffee shops, visiting waterfalls, shopping, and more. I found myself at a talk given by a psychologist brought on board the ship entitled, "Are You Really Angry?"

Well, the title alone was intriguing, and as I listened, I cried when I realized I was, in fact, angry at God for not giving me a child. I had "done all the right things," sought to serve in any way I could, and maintained a "good attitude" about others' success with childbearing. But He had not come through for me! I sobbed in the back of the room, which was filled with others who were also crying, no doubt coming to grips with their own anger issues.

Afterward, I went up on an open deck to get some fresh air. A young lady I didn't know came and sat beside me. For whatever reason, I began talking about what I'd just heard, and she listened with interest. She said, "Why don't you just adopt?" I quickly enumerated the reasons, including that I didn't think I could love another's baby and that it would probably take years. How we didn't have years since I was already approaching the age of thirty-four.

The young woman laughed gently and said, "You're a nurse, right? You're telling me you don't hold these babies here and love them? They're someone else's. And you might be surprised at how quickly adoptions can move."

"Well, yes, I would love them I guess." Continuing with my justifications, I said, "And it'd probably be astronomical in price." The lady was unbothered by every reason I spit out. She was calm and loving. Some of her words penetrated my heart, and then she got up to leave. I asked her name and where she was from. I was stunned as her answer poured out from her lips. She worked at the adoption agency we'd visited a few months ago and encouraged me to fill out the application papers they had already given us. We were on board a ship of about 400 occupants from all over the world, harbored in the Dominican Republic, and she was from the same area in Texas, not far from our home. She had just happened to sit down beside me on the third deck, away from a lot of the activities that afternoon. What are the odds?

The next morning, I reported to my shift and was holding a little brown boy in my arms. He spoke no English, and I spoke no Spanish. He had a nasogastric tube hanging from his nose after having had surgery. Our eyes met, and he smiled the biggest white-toothed smile I'd ever seen. I spoke to him in English, smiling back at him, and he whispered to me in Spanish. That is when I had an epiphany. I said to him, "I could take you home in a New-York minute and love you until the day I die." And then I knew. No matter what our obstacles were, I wanted to be a parent. I knew I could love another's child, and it would be easy to do so.

So, as you can imagine, I rushed home to tell Jon what had happened and asked him if he would still be willing to move forward with adoption. Weary from all of the previous conversations about it, he looked at me and said, "If you don't wait six months more to fill out your application, I still have it in me. But I won't in another year. I'll put this notion away, and we won't have children." I think I filled out my application the very next day. That was in February.

In March, the agency called us in for an interview. In May, we got a call saying that a situation had come up and asking if we would consider adopting a child they thought would be a boy. A month later, we were holding our oldest daughter in our arms, only two days after she was born.

My friends threw me a huge baby shower, giving me everything we needed and lots of support. I decorated the nursery, read books about what to expect in the first year of life, learned what I should do for healthy growth, and complied with all the pediatrician said to do. We weathered colic, allergies, and the unexpected formula intolerance. But we were so enchanted with this little life. I stared at her in her crib for lengthy periods because I didn't want to miss one bit of her life.

It was true what that young woman had said months ago on the boat. I couldn't imagine loving this little life any more than if I'd given birth to her myself. I thought of her as mine; not an "adopted daughter" but simply as my daughter. She was never second best, our Plan B, or less than. Never. I never introduced either of our daughters (another would soon follow) as our "adopted daughters" because I didn't think of them that way. While being grateful to their birth mothers for their sacrifices, I always thought of our daughters as if they were our biological daughters, in every way that meant.

Three years after our first adoption process, we added to our little family by adopting a second time. I was thirty-seven years old. This little life had a magical effect on what I thought might be too old to begin parenting again. She was alert and sported a head full of dark, almost black hair. Her head, perfectly formed, and little body showed me that miracles still happen. Tears glistened in my eyes as I held her for the first time. I felt full to the brim—so completely content. I couldn't imagine being any happier ever again. I think I told God that He didn't have to do anything else for me because this was enough.

From the start, we were open with our girls about them coming "out of someone else's tummy." Gifts came in the mail from their birth moms, and we explained, without using the best grammar, "This is from the lady who you grew in her tummy." The girls understood this. We let them open the gifts and "ooh and ahh" over everything. Because we had a closed adoption, our agency served as the go-between for all of our correspondence. We thought it was important for our children to have minimal contact via the agency but didn't want our girls to be confused about who their mom and dad were. So when we rarely talked about it, we were open and spoke respectfully about their birth moms. I felt that when each of our daughters was ready to meet them, they would ask, and we would help facilitate that meeting through the agency. To me, that thought lived as a tiny reminder that they did not come from our DNA, and I felt regret that I didn't give birth to them myself. But the feeling of sadness quickly faded over time, and we returned to life as usual.

My peers' children were a solid ten years older than our girls, but that didn't diminish my joy in any way. I was so fulfilled, a happy mother of my children. I delighted in teaching them about the world around them and loved homeschooling them until the eighth grade. I loved being the one to influence them and their worldviews in those formative years. During that time, we traveled and were active in the local homeschool community, and reading was paramount in our home. We focused on things like character building and critical thought. I gave 100 percent of myself 99 percent of the time.

When our girls went to public school around the eighth grade, I was active in their school and met other parents who also shared this interest in engagement. They grew up in a vibrant community of music and the performing arts. They both took piano lessons and became quite accomplished. One focused more on voice while the other on dance.

Travel was valued in our home because of the education one can derive from it. Once, while reading the Laura Ingalls Wilder series, we drove up to South Dakota to visit Laura's family farm and some things she detailed in her books. While there, our girls climbed the old cottonwood trees that Laura's Pa had planted, drove a pony that pulled a cart, and dipped their toes in the same creek that Laura describes in *On the Banks of Plum Creek*. Sometimes, I felt as though we had a charmed life because it was so full of things that mattered to me. Tucking them into bed every night and saying prayers was something high on our list of "must-dos." During those moments of quiet came deep thought formulated into words, which I still remember to this day.

Some clouds surfaced now and again during these days of bliss. The clouds I'm referring to are the sudden outbursts of jealousy and discord between the girls. Despite my best efforts at peace-making, there remained an unexplained, underlying tension in the mix. This tension tried to undermine the tranquility I was working toward in the day-to-day. I was bothered by it but dismissed it, telling myself that all kids argue. Because they do.

When they became a little older, the girls participated in camps and workshops, according to their interests. As they grew, they were involved in church and school productions, including numerous recitals and competitions. Some of these things involved travel, which they loved. Our daughters, between the two of them, have traveled to all but five states in the US and to Canada, Mexico, Germany, Puerto Rico, Switzerland, China, Japan, Ireland, Israel, Denmark, Sweden, Norway, Iraq, Egypt, and England. All before the ages of twenty-five and twenty-eight!

Throughout their lives, I've always strived to be in relationships with them at every stage. I taught right from wrong, tried to open doors to the world for them through experiences, and valued what they had to say. I suppose relationship and connectedness are my top values, which was evidenced by the "hands-on" approach I took to parenting. Because Jon had to be gone so much with his job, I tried all the harder to connect with the girls. I expected that we would have a very close-knit family because my family of origin is close-knit. My mother and I had an extremely close relationship, laughing and talking and listening a lot, always sharing in all the ways that mattered. I loved spending time with her before I got married, as well as afterward. She was my rock of encouragement until she passed, some seventeen years ago now. I just knew Jon, our daughters, and I would share this same closeness as they grew and that this would be every bit a valuable thing to them as it was to me.

Jon and I used to say, "Pay now or pay later," meaning if we worked diligently with intentionality at raising them well, we would be filled with joy later as we watched them flourish. We couldn't have known what was waiting, invisibly nestled just under the surface—a surface I didn't even know was there.

Chapter Three

DECIPHERING THE MYSTERIES BEHIND THE VEIL

When one of our daughters was just two years old, she used to love straddling Jon's chest as he lay on the floor to play with her and her sister. She would put her chubby little index finger on his eyelids and talk gibberish. One day, around three years old and on just such an occasion, she said in a very dramatic voice, "I just want to go home!" I was in the room at the time and asked, "What do you mean? You *are* home!" She kept repeating the statement over and over with her little fingers on Jon's eyelids. I was deeply vexed at this and reiterated that she *was* home, and we love her and will always love her. She seemed to enjoy getting a rise out of me and continued for a bit longer. And then, she clicked her heels and said for the last time, "I just want to go home." I then recognized the quote from *The Wizard of Oz* and was temporarily comforted. We went on with our day.

Another time, my sister and I took a road trip with our children. One of our daughters was around four years old. She was in the back seat when my sister offered to teach me how to pay for gas at the pump. (It was new technology, and I hadn't done it yet.) I wanted to learn. She said, "It's so easy. You'll want to do this every time." We got out of the car and left the kids in their car seats and buckled in their seatbelts. My sister showed me how to buy gas. When we got back inside the car, I said to her, "Wow! That's great. I will definitely do it that way from now on." And we drove off.

A few days passed, and I caught this four-year-old daughter in a lie. I confronted her about it and told her that lying was wrong and that we are supposed to be truthful. She looked up at me defiantly and said in her little voice, "You and Aunt Maggie lie." I was stunned!

"What are you talking about?" I asked her.

She told me how she saw us stealing gas. I was speechless . . . and amazed that her brain told her that story and she'd believed it. She had never questioned me about it, just believed that I was dishonest. Sad, bewildered, and even angry, I decided to patiently explain the true story.

She pursed her lips. I couldn't believe I was on trial. I had never lied to her. Still haven't. I was a little indignant that I was having to defend myself to my four-year-old! At the end of the day, it was more important to me that she trusted me than being scolded for thinking such a thing.

The next time we got gas, I made it a point to take her inside, buy her a treat, and go to the counter to pay. While there, I said to the cashier, "Wow, it's sure wonderful to pay at the pump now. That is a great new thing someone came up with."

He confirmed it by saying, "Yes, people really like it." I was absolved for the time being, but the entire ordeal left a big question mark in my soul. *Why* would a four-year-old doubt her parents when we had always told the truth? This one question haunted me without remedy for some time.

As I mentioned earlier, during the first few years of their lives, we would periodically receive gifts in the mail from our daughters' birth moms. The adoption agency scrutinized each package first and then sent it on to us. I found comfort in this and let the girls open their packages as they came. This was always a bittersweet event for me. It was a reminder that I did not give birth to them. At the same time, I coached myself that getting gifts from them was probably healthy in some way, although I couldn't ever think of how that might be.

We used the exact words the agency encouraged us to say. "This came from the lady who you grew in her tummy." They seemed to take it all in stride. I always thought this was weird, though. But they never questioned it; they never talked about it. They just seemed to understand that phrase and go about their lives as they opened their treasures. These gifts weren't especially valued above other gifts but, as with any gift they received, they were happy to open something just for them.

I remember saying nice things to them about their birth moms. I tried to include the soundbites of their stories as we went so we wouldn't be "springing it all on them" as teenagers. But the girls never seemed particularly interested in learning anything about their birth moms. It was as if it didn't matter at all that they weren't in my tummy. So I returned to parenting with gusto and didn't bring up the subject of adoption much after that, as it seemed to be counterproductive. After all, why make a fuss or draw attention to something that didn't seem important to them?

Why continually bring it up week after week since we had "adequately done our part in reporting?"

Through the years, I taught a lot about character and how important it is. I drilled in familiar sayings like, "Gift can only take you as far as character can keep you." We talked of God and His love for the world, the importance of treating others kindly and fairly, and the value of honesty. We took trips together, read every day together, prayed together, and talked about the world around us. I was a very engaged parent because I had wanted them so very much. I rarely felt like a surrogate or second-best. There were only hints of my value as their parent, which surfaced when those big boxes appeared at our door.

There was a time, earlier in our marriage, when Jon and I had considered spending our lives in a remote country somewhere, helping to fly supplies into jungles to aid people without means of getting what they needed for survival. I would coach pregnant women through childbirth as well as provide needed medical supplies. We had the skills to do this. But when we were informed we would have to ship our children off to a boarding school many miles away for someone else to raise, we quickly backed out of that and never looked back. We always felt that if God were ever to give us children, we would want to be the ones to raise them.

I further believe that every child is God's vote that they should live for a time, and each one has a purpose. Every child is a miracle. As a nurse, I know, physiologically speaking, that for all of those factors to come together at one time, it's always a miracle. Do miracles happen every day? Yes. But it came differently for us.

In our lives, infertility became a huge foe. We couldn't scale that wall no matter how many resources we gave to beat it. It was ever-present, laughing at our attempts—or so it sometimes seemed. Making fun of our love for each other, mocking our desire to procreate, our infertility shamed us. Could God have intervened? Of course, He could have. But He chose to create our family differently. The very idea that a loving God would withhold biological children from us later served me in these thoughts. Perhaps, we were to parent these very two! Perhaps, *we* were the best parents for the job, the ones who could shape their little minds and hearts in the best way they should go. Perhaps, *they* would forge our hearts in different ways for how God wanted us to think and grow. And perhaps, together, our little family would touch many others who might just need something we have.

Of course, all that remains a mystery, but we hope (still) to that end. All I can say is that I firmly believe that we did not rescue our daughters. We are not their Savior. We were designed, as were they, to be part of this family for all of our good.

When our daughters came to junior high age, we noticed the usual angst associated with puberty. They were testy, sometimes a bit willful, and sometimes downright cantankerous. There was jealousy. Rivalry increased, as did sour attitudes toward each other. They both loved and excelled in music. One sang, one danced, and both played piano. There were cutting remarks toward each other and less joy in the house than there had been previously. While this bothered me, I chalked it up to normal teenage development.

While they were in high school, I became fatigued. I was always putting myself aside for them in some way. You may say, "Well, that's parenting." I would agree with you at a surface level. But what I noticed were little ways I couldn't say no, even when I wanted to. I waged an internal conflict and asked myself if I was not providing enough boundaries. I had carefully thought through the idea of saying yes to as much as possible, leaving room for decision-making on their parts. I know that came from a place in me, formed from my childhood, because I was more often told no when I had made requests to do something. I think my father feared I would get into trouble, and keeping me home would remedy that issue. Even if he had been correct, I was determined to be different and to extend more yeses to my family's equation. But once our girls reached high school, I felt I was borderline compromised a lot, caught between what I wanted to say and what I needed to say.

It was different with Jon. I have always been able to tell him no when I feel strongly about something. But with the kids getting older, I found it hard to find my voice.

Our daughters differed—like night and day—in their personalities. While one seemed more willing to accept my boundaries, at least outwardly, the other daughter was more overt with her pushback. She was relentless in exerting her will, and I didn't understand why. She would ask difficult things of me—things that required more than I wanted to give. She would ask to go places she knew I wouldn't want her to go. She would ask to have people over and busy herself with activities I felt were not in her best interest. For instance, one time, she reported she'd like to go to someone's house and hang out. I inquired more about what would go on at that house. She finally admitted that they'd come up with a fun game involving chasing each other with cars. When I refused to let her go to things like this, she became downcast and withdrawn. Now, if things had been "normal" in our house, this wouldn't have gotten to me. I could've spoken freely without fear. But there was something invisible living with us that undermined my authority and confidence. With adoption, every word of correction or having to say no felt threatening to our entire relationship. It would be another several years before I would understand why.

As my daughters entered their early twenties, they still had few things in common, and that ushered in sadness. And then it hit me. There's no DNA to bring them together on any level. As I watched the other twenty-something siblings, I noticed there were automatic "sameness" identifiers, which ours did not share. What would that mean in the long run? Would they ever be close, like my siblings and me?

The college years came and passed peacefully. Each break they came home, we saw growth in them and were pleased with the progress. Of course, they were stretching their independence with us, and we were learning our new roles as parents of older children in college. We gave less input unless asked, which worked out fairly well. We attended their performances and helped as needed in various ways. It was a peaceful time because we knew they were heading in good directions and were in wonderful schools in different states. They were happy with the schools and the majors they chose.

It wasn't until graduations occurred that we noticed some drag. Neither of them knew what they wanted to do in life. No relationships, no plans. One came home. The other lived abroad with a mission organization for a year. Neither of them had any direction for their next steps. And we were perplexed. We expected that after college, they would land great jobs and start families. When they came out lacking any understanding about what they wanted to do, the ball seemed to be in our court to help them figure that out.

Simultaneously, one of them entered a relationship with someone who threatened our family in ways like never before. We were truly afraid of what might happen to our daughter, her safety, her mind, and our fractured relationship with her because of him. He had a mesmerizing effect on her soul, and we were seemingly powerless to help her see the truth. His manipulative and controlling behavior met the profile of an abuser. He wanted to take her far away from us, which would've left her isolated from everyone who loved her. To date, this is the hardest thing our family has ever gone through in that it threatened our very existence and, we felt, her life. Right or wrong, we stepped in to save her, as we saw it. Our actions were very unwelcomed by both our daughter and the young man. We were afraid we would lose her forever. A few weeks later, he went back to his home in another country, and she got quiet.

Meanwhile, the other daughter was still living with us and not working, lacking direction. Both daughters, college graduates, seemed paralyzed. They were unhappy and seemingly angry at us for being unable to afford them happiness. Actually, we were all stuck.

One evening, I was attending a class with my sister in another town. We were standing in the parking lot after class, and I fell into her arms in a puddle of tears. All at once, this tumbled out of my mouth: "I can't tell them no or set boundaries because I'm not sure they love me. I'm not ready to sever our relationship, even if it means we're all stuck. I need to know they love me." The words just hung in the air for me to hear again and again while they sunk in.

That was it! The belief that we must keep giving to earn their love was keeping us from being boundary setters.

I'd taught the importance of setting boundaries with others. I believed it was a good idea. But I never saw it more clearly until these moments in the parking lot with my sister. She heard me and questioned it. I couldn't believe that had been the driver for so long in parenting. I didn't believe they would love us unless we were giving. What a heavy load to bear all those years! And now that I was seeing it, would I be able to cut the cord and do the healthy thing? I let that realization sink in all the way home.

I told Jon what I'd seen about the situation, and we both processed it a while. Then we mustered the courage to say to each other, "If we have to keep giving, even though we can't afford it, so that they will love us, it's not real love." I was so weary by what we'd been through, I was ready to lay it down. We determined we would no longer buy into the belief that we could earn our daughters' love, and instead, we set out to offer a more complete love—one that would include both abundance *and* limits.

We began the journey of sharing with them what we could and could not do. It was met with some resistance, but they adapted. Sometimes, I felt as if I'd die if they decided to not love us. We'd poured out our lives for them. I always believed they would care for us like I'd cared for my mom. And yet, this underlying fear always accompanied me in every decision. There were still times when I would say yes when I would rather have said no. I would grant privileges when there wasn't a reason for reward, only to establish credibility for love.

I observed my sister's biological children and how they acted with each other. The girls loved each other and shared in meaningful ways, back and forth as a peaceful way of life. They also related to their parents with ease, and there wasn't the angst we had in our home. Their kids, the same ages as ours, were launched and doing well. So what was the difference? Their circumstances hadn't been as good as ours for much of their lives, and yet, they got along so beautifully.

While this uncertainty continued, things reached a boiling point one day, which resulted in me sobbing in my garage that cold December night after the movie. A few days later, I had the epiphany that if I were to empty the entire contents of my blood and give it to the girls, it would never be enough to overcome the places of pain and struggle I saw in their lives and in our relationship. Over time, I came to accept the fact that I had been a good parent. The pain and difficulties were not my fault; they were something that I could not single-handedly fix. The struggles dove much deeper and spanned much wider than both Jon and I could understand. There was an invisible and uninvited "guest" in our home. Though we didn't know it at the time, we had been dealt a different set of cards from our biological parent peers.

Chapter Four

THE WILD-CARD HAMMER

doptive mom Susan and I would exchange stories about our children. The similarities in our stories continually amazed us. We had adopted all of our children (collectively) at birth. We asked each other, "What are we looking at?" We continued to meet often for a time and found a few resources on the subject. We read the limited number of published books about adoption, and I became even more depressed. This was the first time I bumped up against the term "primal wound." I read a book by Nancy Newton Verrier called *The Primal Wound* and learned so much about what happens in the womb before the adoptive parent ever comes into the child's life.

The author of *Healing Adoption: A Path to Recovery*, Joe Soll, shed light on the missing piece. While I found no redemption in this book for adoptive parents, I came to understand a lot more about what goes on in the soul of the adopted child. According to Mr. Soll and others, bonding begins *in* the womb, not at birth. This is contrary to what I had always believed. While in the womb, the child learns the birth mother's tastes, smell, voice, and essence. When born, this child expects to meet this mother. Instead, they are handed off to someone they're unfamiliar with, and the voice, the smell, and the taste are all different from what they experienced in the womb. Of course, there is no language for them to communicate. If there were, they might say, "Hey, where's my mom?" or "Who are you?" The brain knows the difference, but the baby can't articulate what they're knowing.

Meanwhile, the adoptive parents enter the scene. (By the way, most of the angst shown by the adopted child is directed toward the adoptive mother.) This adoptive mom eagerly reaches for the child, tenderly holds the child, instantly falls in love, and is one hundred percent *in* and hooked. She tells this child that she is their mother, and she loves them.

Since many of us heard that bonding begins at birth with those who hold the child and act like the mom, the mom never knows what's going on in the child. The child is confused but needs to eat. The child is grieving but has no way of expressing it. The wound is caused by what I call "the switcheroo." The brain knows something happened and doesn't have a way of telling anyone. The brain remembers, even though the conscious mind does not. This sets up mistrust from the start, and the adoptive mom is usually unaware of this phenomenon. She goes on and lives as if this child knows no one but her. Therefore, she expects this child to trust her, love her, desire her, and need her.

For instance, I would never have considered doubting my parents when I was a child. It was instilled within me to trust them. There was no reason *not* to trust them. I was their biological child, and they'd never lied to me. I naively expected the same reaction from our children but was met with wariness and suspicion instead. To my daughter's brain, I was an imposter! I had unknow-ingly "switched" her mothers. Once I came to this information, I felt physically sick. Betrayed by what I believed to be true, I felt I didn't deserve this harsh sentence. But this cloudy feeling of loss was so deeply buried inside our daughter, none of us would've known it was there until I started researching.

I began to pick up the pieces of my broken heart and mus-tered the courage to keep reading because I so desperately wanted an authentic and close relationship with our adult daughters. We had told our kids things like they "were chosen" all of their lives. The irony: *we* were chosen. Their birth moms chose us to parent them. Another irony: we had never been dishonest with them, but one of our children often struggled to be honest with us. She told us what she thought we wanted to hear. It was a recurring theme throughout her life. I didn't know why. I have now come to see the psychology behind it.

The process looks like this: the child grows inside one womb and is painfully delivered from that womb. Then they are trans-ferred to someone they do not recognize. They are looking for "the owner of the womb" in which they'd been living, and she is nowhere to be found. They acquiesce to the person who is telling them they are precious and who feeds them. As they grow, they adapt to this new situation. As young children, they are often obe-dient—the perfect children. But something changes as they near puberty. They frequently become argumentative and oppositional.

You may think this is just typical teenage behavior and atti-tude. It's true that this is common developmental behavior for many teens. But with adoption, this behavior comes from a deep sense of shame and the belief that they do not belong or are not worthy of love.

Let me explain further. Very often, the young child is obedient because (maybe consciously, more likely unconsciously) they do *not* want to be given away again. After all, if abandonment can happen once, it can happen again. They will do anything to comply, receive praise, or get noticed and affirmed. This fear of further abandonment is always running in the background. Again, all of this is completely off the conscious grid, both for the children and the adoptive parents. The parents usually have no idea this is going on inside their child. Therefore, it doesn't get named, understood, or addressed at all.

When the child approaches puberty, they want independence like all teenagers, but now, their actions change to test boundaries and commitment. They likely don't realize they are testing their parents' resolve. They poke, prod, and push parents in ways that test their parents' love because that's exactly what they want to know.

"Will *you* leave me too?"

"Is there something I can do to push you away?"

"Will you run when it gets hard?"

"If my birth mother gave me away, then why would *you* stay?"

At this point in my research, I remembered something one of our daughters told me after college. She talked about attending eighth grade in the public school system and being at lunch with her new friends. Somehow, the subject of adoption came up. She endured a flood of questions and comments. One such comment was, "Does that mean they can give you back if you're bad?" She reported to me that she answered, "No. At least I don't *think* so." I was horrified at hearing this, especially when I realized she'd kept this to herself all those years. She had processed it alone. I was deeply saddened to know that in the time between when this occurred and the time she eventually felt ready to confide in me, she had carried this all by herself. That lie buried itself down into her subconsciousness and became a part of her belief system. Not even then did I know what to say to her except, "How ridiculous!" (Hardly a proper response, but I was ignorant of what was going on.)

As an adoptive mom, there were so many instances when I struggled to say no. I felt if I said no, that it would break what relationship I had with her. I never quite felt that she was as invested as I was. I believed I could damage our relationship if I said or did the wrong thing. The root in me, which I couldn't see, was, "I couldn't bear it if she doesn't want a relationship with me. I think I will physically die."

This became the perfect setup for us both to fail. We couldn't talk about this openly because neither of us could see it clearly. It would be years before I understood.

Another side effect of believing they must hustle for their worth can be found in self-sabotage. The behavior can present in habitual dishonesty and risk-taking (like promiscuity, addiction, and other dangerous acts) or lean to the side of fear. Fear of succeeding, fear of failure, fear of not being accepted, fear of evil happening to them—to name a few. Rejection is so big that the dread of it drives the child to "ruin" any opportunity for a connection before it has a chance to begin.

For instance, the adoptee with this modus operandi will begin every new relationship with, "They don't like me." When pressed to come up with a reason, the replies might be, "I'm not their type," "They think I'm stupid," or "They think I think I'm smarter than them." The objections could be as varied as human thought on any subject. The brain is coming up with reasons to protect itself from pain. Having this mindset, the adoptee will often do something unsociable or say something curt, which will, in turn, bring some kind of negative response. That response is then interpreted as rejection. And on and on it goes. Even with a change in location or the names of the characters, the cycle repeats itself. The brain is looking to confirm that they are not worthy of love and belonging. Because they keep getting this everywhere they go, they believe it is true. It is a self-sabotaging mechanism to "keep them safe." According to David Rock's book, *Your Brain at Work*, the brain is mainly designed to minimize pain and maximize reward. So self-sabotage serves them for a time. But at some point, it quits serving them. And, at this juncture, they may seek help through counseling.

Tim and Melissa have adopted three children. Their hearts are as big as the great outdoors. They are both well-educated, have a loving relationship with each other, and wanted to start their family through adoption. They gave their resources, time, and energy to make sure their three children had the best in life. I don't mean opulence. I mean good heads on their shoulders and a good set of ethics. They were proud of their children and felt happy with their little family. Tim spent hours with his son, who ended up playing football in high school. Tim would take him on camp-outs with other guys and their dads; they attended church weekly and had lots of meaningful talks. All was going well until the oldest did the unthinkable. Here is their story:

> **Melissa**: *I suppose I had entertained the idea of wanting to adopt even before I knew who I would marry. Once we got married, we discovered our infertility issues and tried some expensive treatments that didn't work. I more easily moved toward adoption than (Tim) did. It took some time for him to give up the dream of having biological children. He came to see that adoption would not be Plan B but a viable way we could parent.*

Tim: *I think I just needed some time. But I wanted to parent and felt this would be a way we could have a family.*

Melissa: *We adopted three children. We had a private adoption, adopted one through the foster care system, and one was an emergency placement with us through the foster care system, whom we later adopted. (When they came to us) they were three days old, eight months old, and three weeks old, respectively.*

We first noticed some things when our oldest was around three years old. I had a lot of experience working with children as a teacher and had a pretty good idea of what was normal developmental behavior. He would "zone out" or stare into space, seemingly in his own world. There was random "shrieking"—a high-pitched, non-verbal noise. It would always frighten me because I didn't understand what was going on. There would be sudden outbursts and repetitive noises. Another thing we noticed was he wasn't interacting with toys or other kids. He would watch others play but wouldn't play with others or even with his toys. As time unfolded, he would talk to others, but conversations were short and filled with random thoughts. He couldn't seem to make or keep friends because he would do these random shrieking noises or talk about things "off-subject" with what others were saying. He still does this today, and he's now a young adult. When at the playground, he could be found isolating himself, especially when over-stimulated, or playing with rocks. We took him to several doctors, but we heard things like, "He'll be fine." But he was not fine. We knew it. We found a developmental psychologist when he was five and a half, who labeled him as having an "unspecified mood disorder." A long while later, he was diagnosed with bipolar (disorder). He was always missing developmental milestones and had a very tough time handling sensory stimulation. We found out his birth mom smoked heavily and, while pregnant with him, lived where meth was made. She also partook in those drugs and drank alcohol while pregnant. Three different professionals told us our son had fetal alcohol syndrome, which made sense.

As a teen, he always had trouble with peer relationships and found himself on the outside of every circle. He wouldn't engage at all. He seemed to have zero self-regulating ability, instantly going "from zero to one hundred" in his anger and saying very hurtful things to us and others. Once, when he exploded, it was as if he didn't even remember what he'd done. He was "okay."

Tim: *And the weird thing about all of this is that he never learned from his failures. He might feel bad about it but didn't have that internal thing that told him he'd regret this if he kept going . . . (There was no trigger) to change his behavior. He repeated the process over and over as if it were his first time. He just didn't have the ability, seemingly, to self-regulate.*

Melissa: *You know, we just weren't prepared at all for adoption. We had such different expectations. I think we began reading once we started having trouble. We read*

The Primal Wound. *It was such a painful and hard read, but it helped us better understand that this child had already experienced trauma in the womb. We never knew that. Even as an infant, he seemed distant when we held him. Eye contact wasn't coming readily.*

Tim: *Yeah, I'd say reading* The Primal Wound, *as hard as that was to read, was very helpful to better understand what was going on.*

Melissa: *Around seven years of age, we felt we could adopt again. We became foster parents and got training. That training helped us so much. We wished we'd have had this earlier.*

Tim: *In fact, I'd suggest that every adoptive parent goes through this training. We got him speech therapy and occupational therapy through this training.*

Melissa: *We were some of the pioneers for what's called TBRI.*

[For those who are not acquainted with trust-based relational intervention (TBRI), it is a specific approach to raising an adoptee. *The Connected Child* is a book written by Karen Purvis laying out the principles of TBRI. An adoptee herself, she has many helpful ways to speak and act toward the adoptee. Advice on discipline and connection with the adoptee differs greatly from traditional notions of raising a biological child.]

Melissa (continued): *Karen Purvis wrote* The Connected Child *and talked about this way of raising adoptees. The training helped. We got counseling for our oldest at this point. These counselors had been TRBI trained, so that helped a lot. Suddenly, we had resources open up to us, and we took advantage of them. We were so focused on him; we failed to get counseling for ourselves, which would've helped a lot.*

Tim: *Yeah, eventually we got trained in "trauma parenting" and learned that there is prenatal trauma. Unfortunately, our oldest son was already eleven years old by then. But it opened our eyes to adoption trauma.*

As far as how our relationship with our son is now? Well, I'd say it's distant. We feel we've made progress. But pieces of normal development were robbed of us. Because of alcohol and drug abuse, as well as mental illness, we missed so many things we would've loved to have had. Instead of conversations about girls, sports, camping, learning to drive, etc., we were experiencing runaways, ER visits, overdoses, and serial seizures. When he called, we always went and helped him. To this day, our conversations with him consist of what drugs he's tried or what happened in jail while he was locked up. He's seen stabbings. He runs with drug dealers and trusts them more than he does us. He could have just met them and only know their nicknames but will talk about them like they're friends. He has no real relationships. He's gotten a girl pregnant. This makes me so sad that I didn't have the time to teach him how to treat people.

Melissa: *Well Tim, in all fairness, you tried your best, but he wouldn't have it. And he was gone so much of the time.*

You know, he still calls when he gets into trouble. He pretty much has every time. He would say he has a good relationship with us because others have told us this. We're shocked because we don't feel that way. How can you have a relationship with a son living like this?

Tim: *When he was young, he'd throw a tantrum, and I was dismayed. I would try to connect with him by wrapping a weighted blanket around him and holding him tightly. It worked a little, but as he grew, it stopped working. When he first got in trouble with the law at fourteen years old, it was a foolish impulsive decision that I thought we could work through and move past as a family. However, it led him down a path to drug addiction and illegal activity that he chose not to turn away from. These were intentional choices that we could no longer write off as "foolish impulsive behavior" and further distanced him from us and left us in a position where we could no longer help him. But I think I had a facedown moment when he was around sixteen and screamed, "I've ruined my life!" At that time, I tried to connect with him by saying, "Son, you just need to make one good decision at a time and keep going in that direction, one at a time."*

Melissa: *If you were to ask me how I think I've done as a parent, I'd say, early on, that I felt like a failure. But as*

I've learned more, I would give myself a "six," knowing we can't fix him. There's more to this than our parenting. We need to give ourselves a break. He had issues.

Tim: *Yes, I'd probably give myself a "four." The jury's still out. It's truly hard to speak from a place of intellect. I think I did the best I could. But emotionally, I'm still giving myself a solid "four." Something I'm still learning is that self-control applies to my self-talk. I have to be intentional about not telling myself I'm awful.*

Melissa: *Now others who know us and have been supportive of us as parents would say we are an eight, nine, or even ten!*

Tim: *Yeah, they even say, "I want to be like you as parents. You've been amazing! You've been over the top!"*

Melissa: *Counseling has been helpful for our son, at times, I think. We just ran out of options on how to help him. One rehab we found for him, at one point, had him do an exercise. This question was posed: "Who are you angry with?" He could articulate that he was angry with his birth parents. We felt that was somewhat of a revelation to reckon with.*

Tim and I went to counseling for a time because we weren't getting along. This had all been so taxing on our relationship. It helped. I think our oldest learned to play the game. Our other two children have benefitted from counseling. To be fair, we had a lot more tools and resources to help us be better parents for them.

Tim: *Another thing that's helped us is we formed a private Facebook group and invited only supportive friends to it. I can't say enough about how helpful that's been. Even though they weren't adoptive parents, per se, they were always praying and supporting us with their kindness.*

I've noticed that Melissa and I have a bit of trouble with the same gendered child as we are. In other words, the boys and I have more difficulty, and she has more trouble with our daughter. They are both headstrong. And I think our expectations and the ways we would want them to behave as boys and girls affect our feelings.

Melissa: *I wish someone would've told me that despite me trying to love them more than life itself, and doing everything possible to show that love, it still wouldn't be enough. It would've let me off the hook. None of us can fill these holes.*

Tim: *Yes, and I wish I would've read* The Primal Wound *before adopting. My expectations would've changed. I wish I'd talked with adoptive parents to realize perfection cannot be achieved. I think the biggest lie that adoptive parents believe or even hear is, "(Your) Love is enough." It is not! But the thing I hold on to is this: God chose us to be their parents. And He chose them to be our children. A lot had to happen for all this to line* *up as it did. So we pray God will ultimately get through to our kids.*

Melissa: *I'd like to tell adoptive parents to look for other adoptive parents as resources. I can't say enough about that.*

Tim: *I would love to help other adoptive parents. I wish there was some kind of "League of Broken Parents" group. I would also say it's important to better prepare extended family members too. There's a total lack of understanding that also produces problems. Sometimes, there can be racism if the children are of a different ethnicity or race. Even though unacknowledged, it can persist and must be dealt with. Sometimes, grandparents think they could do a better job, and we feel judged. All because they don't understand the dynamics at play.*

When asked what Tim and Melissa would want the reader to know, they responded: *"Don't feel like a failure! It's not you!"*

Jon and I continue to come face to face with adoptive parents who are bewildered with their adult adopted children. They gave and invested heavily, expecting positive outcomes, and have been met with varied ends. Many times, their adult children have gone in opposite directions to how they were raised. While this can be common among biological children, the adopted child carries with them unresolved anger, and they don't know why. It's a nebulous cloud that follows them, and they're not sure of its origin. Even if these grown-up adoptees are educated, accomplished, and seen as "winners," when asked one simple question, most respond like this: "Did you grow up feeling different and if so, why?" Adult adoptees usually start by saying things like, "I love my adoptive parents; there were no problems." As they talk more about their origins, they say, "I always knew I was different but couldn't put my finger on it. I felt I didn't quite belong because I didn't look like my family." Some say, "I thought, 'Why wasn't I worth keeping?'"

Intellectually, the adoptees understand the difficult circumstances of their birth moms, but emotionally, they are unable to justify the reason they weren't raised by them. It always gets back to the emotional belief that somehow their intrinsic worth is at stake. There it is—the wild card! And that question mark around their worth hammers us and them.

It's the unwelcomed, uninvited, and invisible guest named "I am not valuable," which is always present from day one, competing with us, the adoptive parents. And it must be reckoned with. One strategy of war is to know your enemy. I want to interject that *this* is a foe we need to know for us to better understand our place. To know that we are at war with their *lack of understanding of their intrinsic worth* is first and foremost. If we don't know, we endlessly blame ourselves, our adopted children, and or a host of other things. But I would say, most times, we blame ourselves. And it's destructive.

Chapter Five
NAME IT TO TAME IT

I couldn't wait to have a conversation with our daughters. I was learning so much about the intricacies of adoption and the reasons they acted the way they did toward us and each other. We made an appointment to speak with one of them who lived out of town. She welcomed an open talk about adoption, though she'd never really acted interested before and seemed eager to hear what we had to say.

On a decided day, we met at a local coffee shop near her residence. I began the discussion by telling her I'd been studying and researching the subject so that I could better understand some of our issues. I explained I'd learned about these things called "the primal wound" and "the switcheroo." I described what I thought she had felt but didn't have a voice to articulate while growing up. I further explained this might have been the reason she tested me so much. As I spoke, big tears formed in her eyes.

"Wow. This makes so much sense, and I wish I'd known this earlier. It helps."

"I agree, and I told you as quickly as I could because I thought it would help you like it's helped me."

Later, I spoke with our other daughter and explained all I'd learned. She wasn't quite ready to sit and listen, only mildly interested. She was guarded but hung in there. This daughter's understanding of what's been in play has dawned on her a little at a time, in stages. She has been more forthcoming in her feelings as she's felt safer talking about it.

This is one thing I've found to be imperative in our journey as adoptive parents: *We* must make the topic of adoption safe and available to our grown children. The more they see us as okay with the subject, the more they will feel invited into the conversation. If we don't flinch, they won't flinch and follow our lead. We become their safe place—their refuge to say what they're really thinking.

Mind you, this will call forth great courage on the part of the adoptive parent. It takes a lot of steel to stand and hear their words as they work through this information for maybe the first time. Finally, they've been permitted to talk about it. Not only allowed but *encouraged* to go there.

Let me be clear that some adoptees aren't quite ready to trust. They may be internal processors and feel more comfortable "sitting in the back pew" while learning about adoption and all that comes with it. Our job, as adoptive parents, is to reach out and try to create that safe place for them when they're ready. This feels more inviting than forcing engagement. It's all about readiness. When it's on their terms, entering this space we've created can help dissipate the anger in the adult child. Being heard by someone who knows them well is empowering. It may not be pretty at first, but giving them a place to say what they're thinking is both good and helpful to both the adult child and the parents.

I never understood why our children didn't seem to have solid connections with their grandparents, despite the nice things they gifted our kids and our parents' desire to form close relationships with them. One day, to my dismay, one daughter said, "Mom, you know they aren't really *my* grandparents." Ouch. I never thought of that before. I couldn't imagine they wouldn't have a connection with our parents since there were so many gestures toward building those connections. She told me that in thinking about her ancestry, she realized Jon's and my parents did not live anywhere near her, and she didn't feel like they were hers at all. She told me they were *my* parents but not *her* grandparents. One thing that could've influenced her heart was that she didn't grow up around either set of grandparents. Our daughters' main exposure to our parents was when they were both young. At that time, they received much affection from this older generation. When we moved away, Jon's and my parents were no longer part of our kids' everyday world. While we tried to keep them as visible as possible, they, to my sadness, were largely invisible except for the occasional gift by mail.

While this may be a source of pain for the adoptive parent, it may serve us well to understand some key ideas. Unless children grow up around grandparents, there may not be an emotional tie. If they are only working from distant memories (or no memories at all) of our parents, there likely won't be much connection made. After all, our relationship was forged through years of interaction with our parents. Unless there is an ongoing experience or frequent conversations, we really can't expect much of a tie, though we may highly desire one.

On another note, spending time gathering history, as a biological child might do as they grow up, is not common with adoptees, necessarily. Our girls lack interest in researching that information. They seem to feel it doesn't concern them. I've seen this in both of our daughters and have tried all the harder to show them various reasons they should care. In the end, they're just being polite when they listen to my stories because, to them, they are only stories, ones without relevance to their lives.

But make no mistake, they may be seeking their own genetic line. They are trying to make sense of their belonging. How do I know? Because I have talked with so many adoptive parents and adoptees. So far, most of the time, adoptees admit this outright. I am not saying that all adoptees want to meet their biological families. But most have told me they *do* want to understand their genetic makeups, historical origins, and medical histories.

In my research to understand our girls better, I ran across a term called *mirroring*. It is the intrinsic behavior in which one person unconsciously imitates the gestures, speech patterns, or attitudes of another. I immediately understood what this looked like. I've caught myself, in times of deep thought, pressing my lips together. It took a friend to tell me that my sister does the same thing when she's deep in thought. I further remembered that I tend to circle my thumbnail with my index finger for no reason at all. I can distinctly remember my sister, mother, and grandmother all doing this too. I would have never thought of this until I read about this phenomenon of mirroring. It's things like this that connect me to my biological family, without even thinking about doing them. There is so much that I don't have to explain to my biological family. There's already a deep understanding of each other in the silent ways mirrored before me.

The adoptee is scanning the earth to find something they recognize staring back at them. Though the search may be happening in their unconscious brains, they are trying to see where they fit. They are searching for that commonality that is rooted in their biology.

I do want to clarify that mirroring is different from mimicking their parents' behavior. Certainly, humans do take on characteristics and behaviors of their parents based on being with them for years. Things like accents and ways of dealing with problems or joys can be taught or caught. Families enjoy that sense of belonging to each other when they share commonalities. Some say our children even look like us over time. Mirroring is more in the DNA than it is taught or caught. It's unconscious. Subliminal.

I'd like to introduce Melanie. She has a sociable and gregarious personality. She and her husband work very well together, and she is very accomplished in her field.

While she was in our home, we got to talking about adoption, and I mentioned I was writing this book. She confided that she had been adopted. That lead to an interview in our living room, which revealed another story that confirmed what I've heard so many times before.

Melanie was adopted at birth. She grew up in a modest home with adoptive parents who gave her all the love she could want. She and her sister (who was also adopted) were the only children. While she felt loved by her adoptive parents, she always wondered why she felt different. She didn't look like her parents, and her demeanor wasn't the same. She reported that she was more "rowdy" than her demure mom. She sometimes felt like a failure because she just couldn't want the profession, the friends, and the styles her mom had nurtured her to desire. And she rebelled—only for a short time—but mostly grew up wanting to please her parents.

The day came when Melanie decided she wanted to meet her birth mom. It wasn't what she'd hoped for. Her desire to connect did not become a reality. Eventually, she'd also meet her biological father. When she met him, everything came together for Melanie. She felt validated for the first time. Her interests and expertise were identical to his. She shared his humor and his ability to envision things before they were a reality. Her more demonstrative demeanor came from *him*. He had been unaware of her existence and was very glad to have a relationship with her. For the first time, she knew she belonged! The ache she had carried dissolved. For Melanie, her world finally made sense.

While many adoptees pursue contact with their birth moms, neither of our girls are ready to meet theirs, although Jon and I have both met them at different times. We have encouraged both daughters to meet them on their timetable and not a minute before they're ready. We have offered to help them in any way we can when they say it's time. So far, they've not wanted to pursue this. It is our firm belief that adoptees work on their timetable despite pressure from birth moms or any other factor from which they may feel pushed. There are many factors at play and only they know when they're ready. As an accredited life and business coach, I believe we each know, deep down inside, our best, most acceptable solutions to our issues. Sometimes, it just takes the right awareness before we're ready to look at certain things. And that's okay.

———

Elizabeth is in her sixties now. To look at her, one would think she's never had any issues related to being adopted. I have known her most of my life. I grew up knowing and loving her adoptive parents. I grew close to her mother as I matured. Her mother couldn't have possibly loved her daughters more or demonstrated her active involvement in their lives any better.

Elizabeth was a "good kid"—obedient, respectful, helpful, and cheerful. And that was as a teenager! She had the singing voice of an angel and delighted in any worthy challenge. I was a bit intimidated by her, truth be told. But I always liked her just the same. As an adult, she's educated, has had a full career, is happily married, and has three adult biological children. She is well-loved by many and a delight to be around.

We have kept up with each other throughout our lives, and at the lowest point of my parenting journey, I reached out to her one day. I mustered the courage to ask the dreaded questions:

"Have you felt your adoption has presented emotional difficulties?"

"Have you felt loved?"

To my utter amazement and horror, she admitted, "Well, truthfully, every single day, I battle that feeling that I was given away, that there must be something wrong with me, or my mother wouldn't have given me up." She further said, "Don't get me wrong. I love my (adoptive) parents. They've been wonderful. I couldn't have asked for better. But there's always been that nagging voice inside my head. I've battled it and learned how to navigate the emotions of it. So it's not crippling me anymore, but it has always been there. I just don't pay attention to it now."

Tears filled my eyes to hear these words from her! I guess I expected to hear something different because she had never given any hint of feeling this way. Never. And then it hit me that if *she* admits to this only now, how much more a younger adoptee who has never been allowed to speak openly about it must be struggling.

It's not that we didn't allow open speech in our home. We just did not understand the need to talk about adoption. I was going off our daughters' cues, which were largely nonexistent. From where I stood after my conversation with Elizabeth, I realized they were going off our cues. Perhaps they felt the underlying insecurity in me. Not wanting to hurt me, they just didn't want to bring it up. If we'd known then what we know now, I'm sure we would've offered more space for conversation.

In addition, I am now aware of my then insecurity around not being the one to give them birth. Each time something was said about adoption (only in retrospect do I see this), I quickly moved on from the subject because it hurt too much to think they'd need someone else besides me. I suppose I wanted to think it wasn't a triad, but a nucleus family that we were building. To my shock, I was forced to see and accept that all adoptions involve a triad, no matter what the circumstances were that brought them to this place. No amount of ignoring, suppressing, or only giving a polite nod to the subject will ever change that fact. The quicker the adoptive parent sees this, the more likely it will be that they can "set an inviting table" for their young adoptees. When there's a safe, hospitable feel to the space, there's more likelihood for learning to take place.

Chapter Six

BUSTING THE MYTH
OF BEING ALONE

During my many interviews, I witnessed a lot of raw emotion come tumbling out of various parents' mouths. To protect their identities, I have written some of their stories—without names—to help you understand you are not alone, even in your worst moments"

———————

"There were suicide attempts, hospitalizations, many wall repairs due to fists being thrust through them."

"I never dreamed I would feel so alienated from my child. What had I done? Was I that bad of a parent?"

"In the lowest time, I felt like this is as good as it gets."

"I gave my all. And it wasn't enough."

"It was hard every day with my child for many reasons."

"You have to be super strong. You will give love and [sometimes] won't get it in return. Love isn't ever going to be enough."

"I was so sure I could just love these little babies, and we would become this wonderful family."

"We've dealt with rage, sexual abuse, pornography addiction, attempted suicide, and hatred toward me, especially. "

"My own vulnerability shames me. After all these years of verbiage about adoption, now my real heart is exposed! I guess I don't like what I see . . . fear, jealously, selfishness . . ."

"Why am I struggling *so* much with him finding his birth mom? The covenant of adoption seems to have been broken. She is not keeping her promise to respect us as his parents. I did this to myself because I thought it would be helpful for him and for her. When am I going to think about what's best for *me*? See why I'm ashamed? My heart is bad. Christians aren't supposed to think about themselves."

"I'm afraid of being judged by people—good people who don't understand adoption."

———————

Parenting the adoptee can be a lonely journey. When our children were growing up, I was in denial that their needs were any different from biological children's needs. In the day-to-day dealings of household chores and schooling, I felt some loneliness. Because Jon traveled for a living, I was the only resident parent in the house much of the time. I didn't know anything else. I would only look to see how others parented and sometimes felt either sorry for myself or proud of myself, depending on the events of the day. This is no different from hundreds of stories from single parents. The thing I did not realize was how important it was to surround ourselves with other adoptive families. Our children would need it as much as we would. Adoptees carry a certain amount of rejection. Depending on their prior circumstances and experiences, they may demonstrate a lot of that rejection or a little of it. Since behavior is an outcome of our beliefs, the adoptive parent needs to understand what they are seeing.

Here's Sally's story.

———————

... We began looking into adoption because we both wanted so badly to parent. In our early thirties, we heard of a [girl who was pregnant] in her twenties [who was looking at adoption]. We all met at a mutual friend's house to get to know each other a bit and talk about how we would go about adopting her baby and what the terms would be. We did adopt this child and raised him to adulthood.

After we adopted [our son], we went again for more infertility treatments. This time, a viable pregnancy was achieved, and I gave birth to a little girl. Our kids are just over four and a half years apart.

Our adopted son was a model child until about thirteen and a half years old. He went from cheerful, helpful, and kind to mouthy, snotty, and having a bad attitude overnight. I was focused on teenage angst. He pushed away any love. He would say to me, 'Why are you doing this for me? I'm not worthy.' He would never tell anyone he was adopted. He began slamming doors, yelling, and just being angry all the time. I never knew what would set him off. I was determined to not yell in my responses, so I would consciously speak in softer tones. I was always aware that I was the adult and should lead by example. I had only read a couple of books about infertility that had been resolved with adoption. About the only thing they said was that if you can't accept a child's biological differences, then you shouldn't adopt. I wasn't prepared.

Unfortunately, I became a single mom who was going through a divorce. It was a rough time. There were a couple of pastors I knew who were supportive. I read two helpful books. One was Parenting Teens with Love and Logic *by Foster Cline. The other was* The Five Love Languages *by Gary Chapman. I read them through the lens of adoption, and they added another dimension [to my knowledge]. One thing that helped was that I was in counseling (because of my divorce) from the time my son was eight until ten years old. He went to counseling as a teenager for about three years. He was diagnosed with bipolar [disorder] and was put on meds. He didn't take them because he said they prevented him from feeling anything.*

I call those years the "ugly years" because they were so difficult. When I was discouraged, I turned to my faith. I felt God wouldn't have given him to me [to raise] for a bad reason, and I won't turn my back on him.

One night, he didn't come home, and I didn't know where he was. He didn't care if I punished him. I couldn't con-

trol him. When he got home the next morning, I said to him, "You really hurt me when you did that. It stressed me so much." I wanted him to know how his behavior affected me. It seemed to help some. It was like it never occurred to him that I was a person and had feelings. He left home for good at age seventeen.

At my lowest, I felt like I was being destroyed. I had another child I needed to parent, and I was always focusing on him and his bad behavior while leaving her out. If you would've asked me then how I felt I was doing as a parent, I'd have told you, "I am a complete failure." Others, however, would've said, "You're doing OK. You're doing everything you possibly can!"

The things that helped most were getting counseling and reading those books, which helped me understand him better. I repeated to him often, "The decisions that were made were because you were loved, not because you weren't."

Now, many years have passed. We are very close. Someone who knows him well in his life happened to meet me and confided this: "He refers to you now as his best friend." Wow! That was something.

After the "ugly years," I asked him what was it that kept him from being even more stupid than he was back then. Why didn't he get into serious trouble? He told me he always knew I wouldn't bail him out like other parents. He'd have to stand alone, with his decisions.

When asked what she wished she'd known before adoption that she knows now, Sally replied, "It's not like raising a biological child. There's another entire dimension you must help them walk through."

————————

Patty, another adoptive mom, had this to say:

I married my childhood sweetheart when I was young. We'd talked about wanting to adopt someday. But after we married, I gave birth to two children twenty-one months apart. We put adoption on hold and began raising our young. Because of some medical issues, our doctor said it was inadvisable to become pregnant again. Tragically, we lost our oldest in an auto accident at just four years old. Our youngest immediately became an only child at just two years of age.

Two years later, my husband and I met a couple who had adopted children, and they had such great things to say about the whole process. Our earlier desire to adopt was reignited once again. It's funny, but I had always wanted seven children and I thought, "Maybe now was the time to pursue it."

We approached an adoption center near our town. We were contacted and asked if we would like to adopt a little girl and were thrilled and said yes! We never wanted this child to feel they had replaced the one we lost. Instead, we wanted to love this individual entirely on their own merit. Even then, we were thinking about the child. Three weeks after the baby was born, we were notified to come get her. We didn't know where she'd been for those three weeks but were delighted to meet her, hold her, and love her for the rest of her life. Our youngest was suddenly no longer an only child. He was six.

We were over the moon! I knew in my heart that this little girl would be part of our family forever, and there would be no difference between our biological children and her. I didn't think of her as our "adopted" daughter, only our daughter. I would get very upset hearing anything different from those people who felt they had to "educate" me on nature versus nurture.

The agency that helped us with the adoption advised us to tell our daughter she didn't grow "under my heart but in my heart." We were to make adoption part of our normal conversation. When she was quite young, I remember telling her, "We chose you; you grew in my hearts" and other similar things so as not to surprise her one day [with the news] that she was adopted. But a strange thing happened. Every time I'd start talking about adoption, she pushed me away. It was a very definite move on her part, and she didn't like this talk. This continued until she was about three years old. I decided [since] she hated it so much, I'd quit talking about it. I just didn't mention anything more about adoption. Talking about it seemed to hurt the relationship instead of helping us to bond.

When she was ten years old, she asked me what hospital she was born in. I told her I didn't remember. She pushed for an answer and said it was weird that I didn't remember what hospital I delivered her in. Stunned, I reminded her I did not give birth to her and that I'd told her this before. She began telling her classmates at school that she was adopted. The teacher thought she was lying and confronted me. I, of course, told her teacher it was true.

There were real differences between our daughter and me. I was very physically affectionate and wanted lots of touch and hugs. She, on the other hand, wanted nothing to do with physical affection. Her personality was difficult for me. She always wanted to be on the go. After spending the night with a friend, she'd call and ask if the friend could spend the night with us. Always pushing the boundaries of our family, we found ourselves in a battle much of the time. I'd try to discipline her like I had my biological children, and she'd lash out and say I didn't love her or ever wanted her to have fun. She was defiant in the smallest things. When in a "time out," she'd slide down the chair until she was out of it. Pushing. Always pushing. I tried to parent her equally and fairly, but as we lived it, she'd verbally fight us on every decision. It was exhausting.

As she became a teenager, things got even harder. One of her peers became pregnant out of wedlock and told her she'd "never give her baby up for adoption because she wouldn't want them to be like her (our daughter) and not know where she came from." I wanted so much for her to share her feelings with me, but she kept everything inside. When I asked her about her life, she treated me like an intruder. She questioned everything I did and every decision I made. She was quick to instruct me on what and how I should do things or say things. She'd say to me, "I'm never going to be like you! You let people walk all over you, and I'm never going to do that!" She would let my husband help her with her homework. He was strong, and she admired that.

When she was eighteen, she left home and didn't tell us where she was. We were undone with worry and sadness. She had been rebellious for a long time. We stressed the need for her to get counseling, but she refused, saying, "You just think I'm crazy now." Her choice of friendships was less than desirable in that they drank, did drugs, and experienced all that goes with that. We knew she was drinking. But her leaving home shocked us. We were just devastated. I had to admit that I had lost all control.

After several weeks had passed, she got in touch with us and wanted to come back to our town but live with other friends and their parents. This was very hurtful to her dad and me, but she followed through on her plan.

You know, I never thought to get help from any resource regarding adoption. I just didn't know I needed to. I thought that biological children and adoptees were all the same. We didn't know one other adoptive parent in our town. I didn't avail myself of that kind of community, if it was even there. I felt I was a horrible parent.

Just horrible. Others would say I did as well as I could do with her—even that I was a good parent. It's still hard for me to not think I was horrible. If I could go back and parent her again, I would now do things differently. In hindsight, I can see my many failures, but they were done out of ignorance, not from a lack of love and wanting to do right.

Our daughter is grown with a child of her own now. When she was pregnant with her child, she wanted to find her birth mom. After searching, it was discovered that she had died. Many years have come and gone since those days I've described. I'd say our relationship has had its ups and downs. Currently, I'd say we are in a healing stage and moving closer in our relationship.

No matter what you do as an adoptive parent, they [will likely] still feel rejected. It's like they're saying all the time, "I dare you to love me doing this!" Our biological son took correction and knew he was loved. There was never any question about that. But our adopted daughter didn't take correction in the manner it was given. I think it would benefit the adoptive parents to understand how their child receives love and give it to them the way they can receive it. I do believe each child has to choose in their own heart to receive and give love.

―――――――

I want you now to hear from Jack and Cindy. Many of you might remember China's one-child policy, a family-planning initiative that restricted most couples to a single child. Below is their story.

When we were dating, we talked about adopting someday. We felt like there were so many children in the world who needed homes that we just wanted to help. Once we married, we had three biological children in quick succession. We kind of forgot about adoption as we began parenting those three.

At one point, while our kids were still young, there was a big push in the US to adopt Chinese children. Because of the "One Child Rule" in China, there were many infants available for adoption because the parents already had one child. But the rules kept changing. We still had a yearning to adopt and reached out to an agency, and they suggested we look at South Korea. So I looked into it.

We began the South Korean process, which took nine and a half months from start to arrival date. About two months before our daughter arrived, we received a picture of her and fell in love with her at first sight. She was five and a half months old when we got her. She was sent to us with an appointed adoption liaison. This meant that we did not have to travel to Korea and leave our three other children in someone else's care. She had only known one private foster care residence before she came to live with us.

I noticed on the first day that she seemed to cry and cry. I wondered if I'd made a mistake. Would I be good enough? Was I equipped for this job? The first couple of years were rough. She seemed to be grieving. I wondered if it was because she had bonded with the foster mom, and then she got me. Over time, she bonded with me and then finally with my husband.

About eight months after she came home, we discovered she was hearing-impaired. This was probably from birth, but it was hard to know. This began a long journey to help her be able to hear. At two years old, we were told she had almost total hearing loss, and she was given her first hearing aid. At twelve years old, she had a cochlear implant. I drove her to a bordering state to attend a special school where she could get the help she needed. We then enrolled her in kindergarten in our hometown school, where she had a dedicated teacher's aide for two years.

She didn't complain or alter her activities because of her hearing loss. I think she was glad to be able to hear. But all the medical stuff she went through was hard. As a teenager, she wasn't very sociable. She preferred to stay home and read books, and, amazingly, despite her hearing loss, she played piano. She wasn't very emotional at all, and we didn't have the usual teenage girl drama. She got along with her biological siblings very well. They adored her. There was a lot of family support throughout her life. There was a strong bond between each of us. Now that she's in college, she's more sociable.

We never had outside resources on adoption, per se. We were just trying to keep up with her medical needs, occasionally hearing stories about adoption. We didn't have a community around us of adoptive parents. We did read some parenting books—but not specifically about adoption parenting.

We rarely left her with anyone but sought to promote a connection with her while staying home. In the early years, when it was so hard because of the fussy behavior and her hearing loss, I relied on my faith as well as family and friend support. I can remember her saying to us one time, "You're my family." That melted our hearts. My husband would just say, "She's our daughter." He would do anything to meet her needs.

We feel we did our very best with her. I think we gave her a sense of security. Others would say, "She's one lucky girl to have you both for her parents." We would say we are the ones who've been lucky.

There was a time when we experienced a little attitude as she matured. She would roll her eyes at me and pull away some. The differences with the way she relates to Mom versus Dad are that she'll confide more personal things with me, but she respects Dad's advice and input on career choice and academics. She definitely wants his approval.

I would love to tell the readers that this was better than I thought it'd be, although not always what I expected. Love is no different between a biological child and one that was adopted. I often forget that she is adopted. I'd recommend adoption, but I would say to go in with your eyes wide open.

————————

A while back, I had the privilege of speaking with Rick and Shelby about their experience. They reflect on raising their children—adopted and biological.

Shelby: *Those we lived near encouraged us to live outside of ourselves and step up to the needs of others. At that time, there were so many good examples of friends in the area who had adopted, which opened our hearts. I asked myself if I was willing and decided I was. We already had four biological children. We married in 1985, and our kids began to come a couple of years later. When our youngest was six, we adopted a child from China one year older than our youngest. This child had lived in two orphanages before coming to live with us.*

Robin: *When did you notice things about her behavior?*

Shelby: *Well, she was sweet. Her stomach hurt a lot of the time, and she was a very picky eater and had little appetite. She wasn't rebellious but did not know English and that was a problem in that a lot got lost in translation. We weren't looking for anything special, so we missed things that we later looked back on and realized there was more to what we were seeing.*

As she grew into her teenage years, she was very intro-verted and would isolate herself from friends. And then she would get mad at herself for being that way. She had a short fuse and started having bad dreams. She wanted so much to be like her sister, who had many friends and was active—socially. Comparison was a real problem, as was jealousy. Along those lines, our other biological chil-dren were active and good at their various pursuits. This also made her feel like she wasn't good at anything and didn't feel she belonged. Even though she played several instruments and had a way with animals, comparison was a constant struggle for her.

Because of the dreams and content of what she would say, we took her to get counseling as an older teen. It came out then that she had been sexually abused in the orphanage and was suicidal. She made two very serious attempts in the next few years. She had many surgeries and hospital-izations and now bears the scars of those attempts. Her young adult life has pretty much been consumed with this.

We missed so much because we interpreted her isolation and introverted ways as from her being adopted or the fact that she was Chinese. We missed the eating disorder and desire to commit suicide.

Robin: *Describe a face-down moment for you.*

Shelby: *When we found out she'd been sexually abused and when she had a suicide plan. We read books before we adopted but were in total denial. We thought love* *would cover it. We'd been told by others that we'd dodged a bullet because our child was so wonderful. She was very engaging. We didn't see that she was hustling for worth or trying so hard to be perfect. We didn't realize she had been a victim of abuse.*

Robin: *How were you prepared for adoption?*

Rick: *We read books and met with the director of the agency. We certainly had no technical preparation, but we were surrounded by people who had adopted, and all we saw was wonderful.*

Robin: *What help have you received along the way?*

Shelby: *Friends who'd adopted counseled us some, as well as a certified counselor in the work of Karen Purvis's* The Connected Child.

Robin: *Describe your relationship now with your daughter.*

Shelby: *Well, now, she's in her twenties, and I think it's pretty awesome. She asked me, in the middle of all the bad stuff, if I would've known how much trouble she was, would we have adopted her? I told her, "No, I wouldn't have thought I would have the strength for the pain we walked through. But, at this point, I'm glad we did."*

Robin: *What gave you comfort when it was hard?*

Rick: *Hope and faith come alive when you walk through pain. Thinking back, it's been faith—the hope [we had] for the things we couldn't see. We might have to go through the loss of a daughter, but that's when we learned the hardest lessons. Not sure there* was *much comfort in the hardest moments. There were no guarantees.*

Shelby: *I had to just keep my relationship with the Lord, not thinking there was going to be a certain outcome. I took comfort in His character only. I had no other assurances to stand on. That was my hope and strength. I would say I had no comfort but strength. [I knew] It may not turn out like I want. The strength is to just keep going. Our battle with her was to keep holding the truth before her because she believed so many lies. We kept telling her the truth. We kept saying, "There* can *be redemption, you* can *make it, you* can *fight for a good life." And finally, she could accept and believe it.*

Rick: *We don't have a picture of how it's going to end. We gained a perspective of a genuine belief that God is good.*

Sometimes His goodness comes in very, very bad situations, but it is goodness, and it does come. I learned that love is so much more powerful than understanding our grasp on truth. Our faith must be based on our love for the Lord and our assurance of His love for us.

Robin: *When you were face down, what did you do to promote connection with your daughter?*

Shelby: *We pursued a relationship with her. Many times, I had to hold my tongue and not say what I was thinking.*

Robin: *Regrets?*

Rick: *Thinking we could somehow explain something well enough to make her understand, but actually, the victory came in loving her right where she was.*

Robin: *Thinking back over the tough times, how would you describe yourselves as parents?*

Shelby: *Bombing it, not getting anywhere . . . so broken.*

Rick: *Embarrassed at our lack of perception and inadequacy.*

Robin: *How would others describe you?*

Shelby: *You two are great parents!*

Robin: *Describe some of the behaviors you dealt with regarding your daughter.*

Shelby: *Eating disorders and cutting in teen years.*

Rick: *I'm not sure how to describe this but an obsession with certain decisions, as if she was trying to find identity in those things.*

Shelby: *Self-sabotage, wondering why she couldn't just have fun like everyone else. She didn't love touch and was not interested in her ethnic culture or language (because of the abuse which occurred there).*

Robin: *What resources have you used to help yourselves and her?*

Shelby: *Well, certainly counseling. Things that have helped are her getting involved in groups with other women, like Bible studies and recovery groups, which get her engaging with others.*

Robin: *How differently does she relate to Mom versus Dad?*

Rick: *In the beginning, she just wanted to be held by me. Now, we relate in conversations about politics, theology, and more. But she goes to Shelby for emotional stuff or to talk about feelings.*

Robin: *What do you now know that you wished you'd known before adopting?*

Rick: *Love is the answer. The power of love is so much greater than understanding. Realization comes out of that security.*

Shelby: *I'm laughing because I think my answer is that love won't fix everything. It's going to be* hard *no matter* *what! Any child you adopt is a hurting child. But, yes, love is very much a part of it.*

Robin: *Do you think you could've been more prepared?*

Shelby: *No. We didn't have the resources then.*

Rick: *The best tool we had was having confidence in the character of God.*

Robin: *Is there anything you want to say to the reader?*

Rick: *Even with our story, I can say [adoption] is good. I would recommend it to anyone. It's been part of our journey of growth.*

As you can see, each story is a little different but has a common thread. Most adoptive parents struggle over a lack of knowledge and, many times, have trouble finding the education they need. I hope this chapter has helped show that there are many, many people out there who are making their way down the path of raising children who were adopted and feeling alone. But we are not alone. We are an army—a host of people, all who are doing the best they can with what they have at their disposal.

Chapter Seven

DETANGLING THE IMPOSTER
PARENT SYNDROME

W hen trouble strikes, many adoptive parents think of themselves as imposters. They say things like, "I'm in over my
head," or "I should know more, but I don't." Confidence
wanes and doubts creep in. Second guessing becomes a normal
part of the day. What can we do when we feel we've stepped into
an "I'm out of my league" mindset?

Sadie and Mike are both professionals. They married at twenty-nine and knew there were infertility issues but tried infertility
treatments for eighteen months to no avail. They came to believe
adoption was a good option. Sadie tells her journey:

> *We wanted to be parents more than be pregnant. We*
> *were thirty-four and thirty-five when we adopted.*
> *Adoption never takes the place of the loss of getting to*

carry a child inside of you and giving birth. I now give myself permission to not visit new moms in the hospital. Another pain comes up for me when other moms talk about their giving-birth stories. I will tell you about my sister's experience.

We got our daughter, Sarah, at forty-three hours old from the hospital in Florida. The birth mom was fifteen years old. We met her and her mother. We also saw her again when Sarah was [a few] months old.

We got our son, James, when he was eighteen days old. The birth mom was thirty-three and the birth dad, forty-seven. They already had six other children at home and wanted to place him, but the family talked them out of it. They took him home to poor conditions but, later, placed him with us because they wanted someone who'd worked with kids and [had a] medical background. A kind of funny fact is that I had a hysterectomy, and our son was born three days later! He was presented to us on Christmas Day.

We had always wanted children. I had envisioned being a stay-at-home mom and raising kids.

I realized things were different [with kids who've been adopted, compared to] biological kids when our three-year-old daughter cried and said, "I miss my birth mother." She had never met her. On that day, competition was set up in my heart. I felt unworthy and that I could never measure up.

When Sarah was fourteen, we found her birth mother. Sarah was pregnant with her own child, and I drove her to Chicago in a blizzard so she could meet her birth mom. We found her in the hospital in a drug-induced coma. Prostitution, drug abuse, and arrests had been her life. When Sarah saw her like that, she was devastated. I felt better about myself when I saw her in a coma, caused by overdosing on heroin. I'm not proud of that and felt so guilty afterward. At that time, I told myself, "I'm better than a heroin addict!" How awful is that? So now I felt guilty, on top of the other emotions.

Our second child, James, had not had good care and was extremely underweight and listless when he arrived. He responded well to lots of holding and constant attention. Milestones have been met late for typical developmental stages, and he has many learning disabilities, including dyslexia. These struggles continue for him.

Our expectations for our children were to make the honor roll, attend college, embark on professional careers, love Jesus, wear purity rings and stay morally pure, avoid tattoos, and basically be "mini-mes" of us.

We realized we may [need to change our] expectations when our son was in third grade.

Sarah got pregnant twice and is now raising those children. She moved out at eighteen and bought a house at twenty. She's super independent and is working at the dental office and loves it. Her education was varied—

homeschool, a private Christian school, and a public school at different times.

James is currently living with his girlfriend. One by one, our expectations of them have been shattered. James had anger issues, and we had to fix many holes [he punched] in the wall as he grew up.

We prepared for adoption by reading books, going to seminars, and connecting with an adoption agency that offered information.

The resources we used include counseling for the whole family (individually), unloading on three trusted and non-judgmental friends, journaling, and prayer.

My face-down moment came when our son was suicidal and violent. That season lasted for a long time. I was depressed and "menopausal," and he was in our home getting off drugs. We offered to send him somewhere, and he screamed, "No! You'll just drop me off and never return for me!" We knew we couldn't take him anywhere, that he'd have to stay with us.

The thing that has helped him get better is that he met a girl worth knowing. She is a Christian and told him to choose drugs or her. He chose her and still does.

I think we've done a great job with our children. The kids love us, and we've kept their hearts.

Others would say now that we've done a great job. But there was a time these same well-meaning friends were judgmental, and we felt the judgment while our kids weren't doing well. Now, we receive compliments.

The thing that comforts me is that my kids love me and want to hang out with me. Sarah's worst fear was that I would give up on her.

James is closer to his dad now. Sarah calls me every day. They are close to both of us.

What I now know that I didn't before is this: It's OK to have a little grief over my loss, my inability to become pregnant and give birth. I didn't know I'd feel in competition with my kids' birth moms. And then the guilt over my own emotions regarding the competition with birth moms.

I'd now say don't expect them to be "mini-mes." I thought it'd be 70 percent nurture and 30 percent nature, but now I think I'd flip that—at least while they're being raised. Then, it seems to have flipped again. I would've gotten more counsel. I would let go of expectations for myself and my kids.

James met his birth mom and siblings behind our backs. There have been drugs and jail time within his biological family. One of his "bio sibs" told him, "You need to thank God every day you got out of this family and had the love you did!"

Both kids love their adoptive grandparents.

Sarah fantasized about her birth mom. But she also fantasized about being our biological child.

Klonopin (a psych med) has helped James. Prayer and instrumental people in their lives have helped too.

We have come to believe and act upon the advice, "Go after their hearts, not their behavior." This allowed us to weather the judgments put upon us by others. Mike always says, "Character trumps curriculum."

————

I have firsthand knowledge of Ruth and Bob. I've watched them parent their children for years and found them to be very loving and generous. I'm so glad they've chosen to be courageous in telling their adoption story. It demonstrates the power of tenacity amid doubts.

Ruth: *We'd always talked about adoption. Bob was adopted by his dad. I had five cousins who were adopted. We just always left the door open.*

Bob: *We had a few infertility issues but finally could conceive with meds.*

Ruth: *After our first biological child, we had more trouble conceiving again, and our doctor asked if we were interested in foreign adoption because we could get a* *baby sooner. So we went in that direction. We brought Lila home at seven months old. Shortly afterward, we had another biological child. And because we didn't want Lila to feel different, we adopted two more, who shared the same nationality—fifteen months apart from each other. So we had five children spanning ten years. We wanted to adopt because we wanted to build a [large] family. My cousins who adopted their children from birth had no problems with their children and we felt we could give lots of love and everything would work out just right.*

Robin: *When did you begin to wonder about what you were seeing?*

Ruth: *We took Lila to counseling when she was in fourth grade for what we thought was RAD [reactive attachment disorder] because she had trouble making and keeping friends; there were always issues with other kids at school. Once, in first grade, she hit another student. But we thought maybe she was just strong-willed.*

I want to interject here that RAD is a diagnosis that is given to children who have typically been deprived of physical affection, such as holding and comforting, within the first few months or years of life. We will go into more of this later in the book.

Bob: *She [Lila] did a lot of comparisons—herself to others, especially her older brother. She never felt like we treated him the same, that she always came up short. We found the reverse was true. We probably went overboard* *the other way to prove she was equal. Her memory was very skewed about how she was treated. In eighth grade, she had self-esteem issues, which resulted from the bullying she experienced for being Asian. We talked with the school many times about the bullying and took her to counseling. In high school, she'd hop from friend to friend and would spend time with people we thought weren't great influences on her. She would spend time with boy after boy but denied she was dating even though they would go to movies or eat out together.*

Robin: *How were you prepared for adoption?*

Ruth: *I stayed home to bond. I wouldn't leave them in the nursery so they would bond with me. We took classes given by the adoption agency to prepare for the early days of getting them home.*

In the eighth grade, we took Lila to her native country because she kept saying she didn't belong with us and wanted to go back. Once we got there, she said, "I look like them, but I belong with you."

We also went five or six consecutive summers to Culture Camp (specifically targeting the country of her origin), which she didn't like, so we finally quit. We accepted a foreign exchange student from her country of origin, thinking she'd bond and learn about her birth culture. Instead, she couldn't stand this girl. It was disastrous.

Robin: *What help have you gotten along the way?*

Bob: *Nothing. We tried counseling, but she quit talking to the counselor. She was a nineteen-year-old stuck with a fourteen-year-old mindset. She wasn't maturing.*

Robin: *Describe your relationship now.*

Bob: *Rough. She was found guilty of molesting a fourteen-year-old student at the high school where she worked. She was nineteen and dating a great guy who we liked. But she was arrested, found guilty, and put on the sex offender registry for ten years. She could no longer live in our home, have any contact with other children, or spend the night with us. She had to get an apartment on her own. She's struggled to keep jobs, often living from boyfriend to boyfriend. In high school, before this happened, we became aware that she'd hooked up with many guys she'd met over the internet. We thought we'd talked through most of this behavior with her, and she had moved on. But now this!*

Robin: *What gives you comfort?*

Bob: *Well, we have a very supportive staff at our church and other adoptive couples who've been generous with their time and listened to us process.*

Robin: *Describe a face-in-the-dirt moment.*

Bob: *Well, I felt like my life and ministry had ended. Complete failure. What had we done? I think the real-ization that we've tried to demonstrate love, talking* *through things, be positive . . . and then for her to feel so low about herself that she's willing to find affection in all the wrong places, that she is willing to take whatever comes and feels undeserving of good things . . .*

Ruth: *Definitely the true sexual charges and subsequent arrest. I thought we'd come through the worst of it and then this. I almost had a nervous breakdown. I couldn't breathe. I kept asking myself what had we done wrong? Why is this happening?*

Bob: *The biggest struggle, the common thread through all of our adoptees, is they just don't feel like they ever fit; they have a hard time coming to grips with who they are. They see themselves from such a different view.*

Robin: *In the face-down moments, what did you do to promote a connection?*

Ruth: *We just showed her love. We hugged her, attended all court dates, waded through the very difficult Snapchat pictures online, and just kept supporting her.*

Bob: *The good boyfriend disappeared. She's always said we weren't supportive. She's a very selfish, self-absorbed, and self-focused individual.*

Robin: *How do you feel you did as a parent?*

Bob: *Well, I believe God gave us this opportunity, mission, to raise these kids who aren't our biological kids. It's* *not over yet. God gives us what we need. We just keep loving them the best we can.*

Robin: *On a scale of one to ten, ten being awesome and one being horrible, where do you fall as a parent?*

Bob: *A five.*

Ruth: *Bob is* certainly *more than a five!*

Robin: *What would others say?*

Bob: *They think we're amazing—over the top.*

Ruth: *Then why isn't it working?*

Robin: *What are some resources you've found to be helpful?*

Bob: *A couple of adoptive couples have listened to us.*

Ruth: *Youth pastors have reached out to our kids and tried to make a difference. Counseling has helped me, not them so much. Kids pushed back against counseling because it made them feel like they were bad—a stigma was attached. One of our adopted sons had a suicide plan. We took him home to school him because of that. He hated school. He was always drawn to the darkest thing and everything we don't believe in. We are still homeschooling him.*

Ruth: *We got counseling out of desperation of struggling with life issues, we got to the end of our expertise and thought a trained person could do more . . . maybe our kids would listen to someone else.*

Robin: *What are the differences in the way your adoptees relate to mom versus dad?*

Ruth: *Daughter and I are like oil and water. She goes to Bob for everything. I can do no right.*

Bob: *She lies a lot, and I'm not sure she listens to me either. Our one boy is autistic, so he's in another category altogether. The other adopted son relates equally well with both of us.*

Robin: *What do you now know you wish you'd known before adopting?*

Ruth: *Don't go in with rose-colored glasses and believe that loving on them is going to make the difference. Even from birth, there's something that's there. They're going to struggle. Don't believe that 'if I just love [them], it'll all be good.' Be realistic. The agency lied about one of our adoptees, saying they were on task with their age group. We had no idea about autism and developmental delays. Maybe we could've taken some classes on reactive attachment disorder had we known about it ahead of time.*

Bob: *We have done our very best to love all of our kids equally, but our adoptees have struggled with things our biological kids don't. My heart breaks for them.*

Robin: *How many times were they moved before they came to you?*

Ruth: *First, the womb, then a foster care situation, then an orphanage for most of the time, and then they came to us.*

Bob: *The boys were in the womb, then in one foster house, and then us.*

Julie and her husband, Peter, have four biological children but wanted to adopt for as long as they could remember. Their story serves to remind us we aren't "fixers"; rather, we are real parents.

We had the idea we wanted to open our home to whoever would need a home. As Christ-followers, we just wanted to help anyone who needed help—and we felt adoption would be a great way to do that. We both had come from broken homes. I had come from foster care myself and know how rejection feels, especially from a birth mom. Because of what I lived through, I felt it would help me understand our kids more. I never got to meet my biological father before he died, and that's always been a sad thing for me.

Both my husband and I felt we were pretty ready to take on whatever came our way through adoption. We were twenty-eight when we started the process but kept getting turned down because we already had four biological children, and we were considered young. We served in respite care and emergency foster care. One day, an agency in another state called us to see if we were interested in taking a sibling pair. We said we were, but we probably wouldn't qualify since we had tried before. In the end, the agency placed the siblings with us when the kids were seven and eight years old. Some years later, we adopted a third child with medical issues.

Right away, I noticed things were going to be hard. The agency educated us on our children's biological history, and we went in expecting the unexpected. One was vicious. One child purposely peed the bed and wouldn't tell us for days so it would smell. Both children defied authority and were unkind. There were frequent meltdowns. Over time, I have realized that love isn't enough. It's tons of consistency with that love that can make things different.

We haven't had what you might call "a support system." That said, one of the best things we did with our one child was to enter her into a RAD facility where she was away from us for nine months. The workers there were trained and so good with children who'd been passed around a lot. We visited her every week. And we lowered our expectations. She kept saying she wanted to meet her biological siblings. Since there had been no meltdown in a year's time, we thought she was ready. She wasn't. Things got awful from there. The meanness toward me continued, in addition to her saying things like, "I want to die." The facility began [medication treatment] for our child, and got the meds regulated over time, as well as therapy by licensed counselors. Somewhere around six months into the stay at the RAD center, she was belligerent, and I just couldn't take it anymore. I got up and said, "I've always been here for you. I've come weekly for the past six months, given you love, and accepted you. I can't endure you treating me this way anymore!" I walked out, leaving the therapist and my child in the room. I'm not sure what the therapist said, but our child changed for the better after that day. At about the seven to eight-month mark, there came a weaning period toward home. First, there were day visits, then overnight stays at home, then weekends. Now, all seven children live at home with my husband and me. Currently, our adoptees are doing well.

At my lowest point, I watched helplessly as the ambulance took our daughter from our home to a lockdown unit. My husband and I felt like failures. We were afraid of what would come next—if we could be the parents she needed and more. We had been lied to and felt so vulnerable. My worst pain was the realization that I couldn't make her love me.

The thing that gives me comfort is the hope of their futures as adults with their own families. They get to start over with their kids. I love to watch our biological and adopted boys get along.

Early in the adoption, our son acted out but said, "I didn't like the way I felt after I was mean to the foster mom, so I quit." Later, when I asked him why he didn't yell and scream like his biological sister did, he said, "I used to pray for a family every night. Even on the worst day here, it's still the best day."

There are some differences between my kids. My biological kids love to snuggle. My adoptees do not. It must be on their terms, if at all. To promote connection with our daughter, we let her go to public school because she needs a break from us. I homeschool the others but let her go to public school to have some autonomy. She seems to relate to us better at the end of the day because she's had other experiences and been around more than just us.

In my down times, I never know if I'm doing the right thing. It feels like things are constantly broken. But I think we're doing a pretty good job of parenting because we have lots of great conversations with the kids, and they want to come to us. I think those that know us best would say our parenting is "pretty good."

Our daughter doesn't take advantage of the licensed counseling we afford her but does seem to appreciate the opportunity that it's there. She is still on meds. I worry she may not take them or can't afford them when she grows up.

Peter and I have a great marriage. We talk about everything. Our adopted son doesn't like to talk much, but my husband will be very intentional with him, drawing him out. He will come to me more than his dad. Our daughter talks more to her dad and accepts discipline better if it comes from him. She has a very resistant heart toward me; often, she won't talk to me much at all. She looks to me for praise and appreciation. She wants to please me—seemingly.

I wish I'd known that we weren't going to fix anything with adoption or love. Those things weren't going to be enough. I now think it's a lifetime of trying and loving. I think we just have personalities that tend to think, "You get this one moment. Make the best of it." If I hadn't adopted, I wouldn't have known how great it is. In addition to the greatness, I now know we can't fix anything.

Chapter Eight

WAYS TO NAVIGATE ABUSE AND NEGLECT

Each adoption is different. Adopting at birth is less interruptive for the child than an international adoption or the adoption of a child who has been passed around multiple foster homes and orphanages. But each adoptee comes with a past. Even if it's a nine-month stint in a womb, there are many things going on, and they probably won't be able to articulate them even as they grow.

Adoptive parents' expectations are usually high. There is typically a belief that says, "I'm going to do so much better than *my* parents." Before the child arrives, there are many dreams and fantasies about what the child will look like, act like, and activities in which the family will indulge. Because the adoptive parents' expectations run high, they may even expect gratitude from the adoptee. Many agencies believed and told adoptive parents these babies "are a clean slate" and just "go build your life" with this child. Unknowingly, adoptive parents take the child home, parent like they were parented or even try to do better than was done to them. They are not told these children have a past. They are not told these children will struggle with rejection and may even have a hard time bonding. Certainly, not every adoptive parent has experienced this, but many have.

Many young children found in orphanages or passed around the foster care system often seem charming and win their parents' hearts quickly. What parents need to know is these children may have a hard time attaching, despite what their engaging interactions with prospective parents show. They have learned to be engaging with everyone. The parents may mistake this as true attachment—love at first sight, if you will. Truth be told, these children may treat everyone the same way. They will need a lot of love and intervention.

This is a good time to talk about reactive attachment disorder (or RAD). It is a diagnosis involving all sorts of severe behaviors, acting out coupled with anger, especially toward the adoptive mom. These behaviors come from a place in the child's psyche that believes, "I was abandoned once; now I'm untrusting of you and will push you until you break and reject me too." Children with RAD have been left without proper affection, comfort, and physical tending to for their emotional needs. According to the Mayo Clinic, children who have RAD can form attachments, but this ability has been hindered by their experiences.

There is hope. It is my privilege to introduce to you some doctors and therapists who have expertise in different areas.

Meet Heidi. Her qualifications include a Master's Degree in Social Work (MSW), being a licensed clinical social worker (LCSW), being a Certified Daring Way™ facilitator (CDWF)—which is training in the work and research of Dr. Brené Brown—and she's a single adoptive mom. The following are her words in a conversation we had recently.

I wear both hats every day. I thought I was prepared but still feel out of my league. I feel like I'm never good enough. I never go a day without switching between therapist mode and mom. I have a heavy background in attachment disorders and a lot of certifications, degrees, and training. But when it's your kid, it's different.

At the time I adopted, I had the normal expectations of parenting. Of course, there would be challenges. I could see minimal attachment problems, but we were just two peas in a pod. At eleven months old, he wouldn't sleep and had acid reflux. We later found out he was allergic to dairy. He was hyper-vigilant but also affable, playful, and joyful.

I had grand plans for attachment parenting. But he would have none of it. He would say, "I need you." That would soon be followed by, "Go away." Intellectually, I understood, but emotionally, it was very troubling—sad.

In all my studies, I knew of Dr. Peter Levine's work with trauma and sensory integration. We know that the brain develops top down, inside out, organizing around patterns that are happening. I conceded I needed help. This brings up shame even now, as I'm telling you.

He's always been hyper-reactive to loud noises. When he was four years old, I took him to a prenatal therapist. It was a disaster, a terrible fit. My son has been to four or five therapists. I just kept going until I found a good fit.

I highly suggest that to anyone who finds themselves at a loss in this area, keep trying.

I tried every modality. My son's rage began at age four and took on more strength each year. As he grew older, he quickly became more than I could handle. I was fortunate enough to know a therapist near me who uses neurofeedback. We had actually tried this before, albeit largely unsuccessfully, but something told me to try again with this particular therapist. I took my son in and remained a little cautious but wanted so badly to get him help.

Neurofeedback is a process by which electrodes are placed onto the brain for a specific time. This stimulates parts of the brain. Old pathways are dislodged to make room for new ones. The brain becomes smooth and less rigid. I can't believe the differences I'm seeing in him and in such a short time. Others have asked what is going on because they see a real difference in him; he's just more settled. The episodes of rage have greatly diminished since the neurofeedback began. His [medications] have been cut in half because of this treatment. He says he feels calmer and wants to be close to me now. He's more connected to himself, others, and me.

For those of you who would like to learn more about neurofeedback, check out this resource: Sebern Fisher's *Neurofeedback in the Treatment of Developmental Trauma: Calming the Fear-Driven Brain*. There is so much in this book about how neurofeedback helps the brain heal and find peace through understanding circuitry, frequencies, and rhythmic oscillations. (That's fancy talk for how the brain works.) She talks about the great help it gives to those who are suffering with the effects of child abuse, neglect, and abandonment. To find someone in your area, you may have to do some digging, but it may prove very helpful.

———

Recently, I spoke with Dr. Pamela Bell, EdD, LPCC, LPC, NCC, Board Certified Neurofeedback Senior Fellow, BCIA, at the Neurofeedback Center in Dallas. She informed me she has had excellent results with neurofeedback in those diagnosed with RAD. While these children missed the coddling we need in infancy for the brain to develop fully, these treatments essentially "correct" the EEG.

> **Dr. Bell**: *There comes a point in which it is advisable to decrease the patient's meds for them to not become toxic because the neurofeedback is working. Many times, the psychiatrist is uninformed about how this works and is adamant about increasing the meds because of the patient's agitated state. These conflicting ideas between professionals can cause the parents to stop these very important sessions. But those who continue with the sessions and decrease their meds when it's time have had great results. They become calmer, are more likely to improve socially, and even complete higher learning degrees, as well as discontinue the meds altogether. It is gaining ground in the professional world now. I now have psychiatrists recommending me to their clients.*

I asked her where our readers can find a qualified neurofeedback practitioner.

> **Dr. Bell**: *Make sure they're board certified with the BCIA (Biofeedback Certification International Alliance).*

———

Additionally, I spoke with Dr. Wes Center, PhD, LP-S, NCC BCPCC, BCN. To better understand his expertise, I'll list some of his accomplishments. He is the president and clinical director at Focus for Living and a licensed professional counselor. He holds a Master of Arts degree in Marriage and Family Counseling, a Master of Arts degree in Christian Education, and a Doctor of Philosophy degree in Psychology and Counseling. He is a Board-Certified Professional Christian Counselor, National Certified Counselor, and board certified in Neurofeedback.

He's been working with adoptees for close to fourteen years in the area of neurofeedback. He works with kids who have ADHD, autism, and particularly adoptees who have been diagnosed with reactive attachment disorder. He told me that with kids who had RAD, he saw roughly a 94 percent improvement in the reduction of symptoms.

> **Dr. Center**: *The clinic performs a neurocognitive assessment test, which covers about thirty different things, including cognition, verbal memory, and vision memory. Many problems improve for the child that were not previously on the parent's list of concerns when they brought the child into the office. Because of testing throughout their time with us, we can measure improvement all*

along the way. For instance, a parent may bring a child in because he is aggressive or acting out in other ways. In the course of treatment, he may also receive help with learning disabilities that were unknown to the parent.

Robin: *When is the optimal time to begin neurofeedback?*

Dr. Center: *When parents first see signs of acting out or when they're diagnosed with RAD, they should begin treatment. The earlier the intervention, the more quickly one can see results. We have worked with young adults with RAD who've never gotten any interventions before coming to us and have gotten great clinical outcomes.*

Robin: *What kinds of improvements have you seen?*

Dr. Center: *First, we see improved sleep. They wake up rested without an alarm clock. These kids progress to being able to be happy, accept a compliment, express themselves positively, be proud of themselves for an accomplishment, smile, etc. They have appropriate affect responses. They understand the nuances of a joke, for instance. They become more emotionally astute.*

Robin: *How long does it take to see improvements?*

Dr. Center: *In as little as five to ten sessions, we see sleep improvements. For some, it takes up to fifteen sessions to see improvements in affect, emotional regulation, and control.*

Robin: *What is the typical protocol for kids with RAD?*

Dr. Center: *We see them two to three times weekly for one-hour sessions. The duration of treatment varies, depending on the parents' goals. On average, the treatments run from forty to eighty sessions total, but some go much longer because they are seeing improvements and have definite end goals in mind. For instance, one client was non-verbal when he came and is now speaking. We have others who begin treating while staying with an at-home caregiver [and homeschooling] and progress to attending a mainstream classroom. I've seen an older teenager come in with severe gaps in learning, such as being unable to subtract and add properly. After doing neurofeedback for a while, he is now doing age-appropriate algebra. He has been coming for treatments for a year and a half.*

Robin: *What are some accompanying treatments you use to enhance neurofeedback's success?*

Dr. Center: *In the beginning, every kid is given a neurotransmitter stress hormone test as well as functional genetic testing. Many of them come from other countries with different soils and diets. I proceed with looking at gut health because a lot of issues actually begin there and are masked by behaviors. We usually run a food sensitivity test to find out what is inflaming the gut and have the kids omit these foods for about six months and then slowly reintroduce them. Many times, these kids only eat a few things and, over the long term, become sensitive to* *them. We may have them take a prebiotic or probiotic if it's warranted. We look at their stress hormones and other things. We practice play therapy, pet therapy, and talk therapy in our office. Talk therapy is teaching them to express themselves with words instead of fists. We work on verbal tone and mindfulness in how the words sound when they speak. This integrative approach adds to the overall success we are experiencing.*

Robin: *And what about meds?*

Dr. Center: *Yes, all are on meds when they come. There are natural psychiatrists who work to get them off their meds. One I can recommend is Dr. Brian Dixon, MD. He's a Board-Certified Child and Adolescent psychiatrist who has had success with getting kids off their meds over time.*

Robin: *Does insurance pay for neurofeedback?*

Dr. Center: *No. The reason they give is that neurofeedback is an experimental treatment. The fact is neurofeedback has been around since the 1950s. EEGs have been around since the 1930s and are still being used. EEGs are covered by insurance today. The facts are that there is less evidence to support the efficacy of SSRIs (meds) than there is to support neurofeedback. But the reasons for covering what they do cover are wrapped up in public outcry and keeping their constituents happy. Therefore, meds are cheaper than treatments like neurofeedback because they're covered by insurance companies.*

Robin: *So how much does it cost?*

Dr. Center: *Depending on the parents' goals . . . three months could cost $4,500–$5,500. To complete a protocol might run $7,500–$11,000 for about eighteen months of treatment. I want to say here that we typically will treat for three months or longer and then take breaks. I've seen kids do well when the parents take a break. They come back when the kid has new issues, such as drug use, promiscuity, or some other behavior, which they weren't demonstrating before. It also gives the parent a break financially on those "off" periods. But neurofeedback helps at that juncture too.*

Mixed modalities are best to help the dis-regulated child. We teach parents behavioral interventions, emotional regulation strategies, and cognitive monitoring. We also can't dismiss our fallenness. We all have a need for grace. We are broken physically, emotionally, nutritionally, [and in other ways]. At our clinic, we teach parents how to work with their children. We also emphasize teaching parents to deal with their own stuff so that it doesn't complicate their children's issues. I have play therapists, a pet therapist, an LPC (licensed professional counselor), a kinesiologist, and a nutritionist all here under one roof.

Robin: *Is there anything else you would like to tell our readers?*

Dr. Center: *Yes. There is a non-profit in Fort Worth [Texas], who does much of what we do. They work with* *children who have been neglected or abused. You can find them at fosterthemind.org, and Brian Butler is trained in brain-based therapies.*

Another thing I'd like to tell the reader is we have a high population of evangelical Christian parents who've thought that love was the only answer for their child. They've adopted, many times, several children from other countries with heavy metals in the soil, birth moms exposed to alcohol and drugs that they were unaware of, and more. These kids are going to need more extensive help than just love. Here at the clinic, we support kids and their families. We work with the entire family. Sometimes, these kids think of themselves as "the problem." The truth is the kid has *a problem; he's not* the *problem.*

I liked what Dr. Center said. It's easy, sometimes, to feel as if our precious children *are* the problem. While, in our wiser moments, we know this isn't the truth, we may become worn down from all the pushback we get and default to this belief. This, when believed, can have some not-so-good outcomes. I am thankful for these words of hope. What a good reminder of what is true.

In my humble opinion, I believe that if counseling is sought, it would be best to retain someone who is experienced with adoption and all the issues which are at play. There are many types of therapy out there that have had great success in adoptees of all ages. Let's hear from some more professionals.

Beverly Kline, at the time of this interview, is the founder and executive director of Living Alternatives in Tyler, Texas, a private 501c3 that works to empower women and meet all kinds of needs. She has worked with birth moms from 1982 to the present. The scope of what they do is vast in that there are several "arms" of the organization. The different departments do things like pregnancy testing and sonograms, parenting classes for new moms, offer a home for pregnant clients, complete with a "house mother," and there is a store with brand-new donated clothing where clients can spend points for goods. The adoption arm of the organization is called Loving Alternative. Beverly talks about her familiarity with a popular therapy called TBRI.

> *About six years ago, I became acquainted with TBRI (trust-based relational intervention). We have suggested this to our adoptive parents. The companion book is* The Connected Child *by Dr. Karen Purvis. The premise is that adoptive children are different from biological children and need different things from their parents. The idea is to bond, to attach. Many of the normal ways of dealing with biological children don't work with adoptees. There is already a sense of rejection from the birth mom's placement of the child and being sent to their room feels like banishment. Of course, that is not the adoptive parent's view of the situation. TBRI goes into depth about establishing trust, keeping the child close, and being patient.*

Kay Holler, MSW, a licensed clinical social worker in Chicago, Illinois, has worked with adoptees and their parents for over two decades. She has vast experience with the various issues that occur around adoption. Her information is on the additional resources page.

I reached out to her a while back, and she answered my questions from her perspective. She had this to say:

> *In my experience of working with adoptees and their parents, I see a theme that ties in all stories of adoption together. I'd say they need to have a coherent life—the need for connection.*

> *Out of those I've worked with, I've found about 10 percent were adopted at birth, approximately 20 percent during the first year of life, and about 70 percent after the first year of life.*

> *In my estimation, about 80 percent of the adoptees have an intellectual knowledge that they're loved and are worthy of love and belonging but "feel" the opposite is true. Some of the main reasons clients come to me are for attachment difficulties. These difficulties can manifest in behavior problems, like lying and stealing, emotional outbursts, school-related issues, attention problems, and identity and reunion questions.*

> *There is a range of attachment-related difficulties. I'd say RAD is more on the extreme end of the continuum of attachment difficulties. It's a very strong term. Most struggle with some degree of attachment difficulty. I have worked with those adopted at birth who struggle with attachment issues, though not ones with full-blown RAD who were adopted that young. Some of the current modalities in treating destructive behaviors like insecurities, anger, mistrust, and self-sabotage are Theraplay*

(a relationship-building psychotherapy), DDP (dyadic developmental psychotherapy), and TBRI (trust-based relational intervention).

I think training the parents to act in new ways helps the most. I'd say about 75 percent of adoptive parents are completely unaware that their adopted child most likely has trauma issues that biological children do not face. Encouraging the parents to do their own work is paramount. Healing their own past traumas and modeling new ways of acting with their children helps to unlock hearts and enables them to move forward.

I see many adoptive parents who are discouraged with what they're experiencing with their children. I tell them to hang in there. Love does not conquer all. These children take longer to mature, but they do, eventually. I'd like to encourage your readers to join a support group for adoptive parents. They can call the adoption agencies in their local area, and they should have a list of resources. Also, adjust your expectations. This child will not be like you. Celebrate small movements toward maturity. Keep the connection with your child no matter what.

Most adoptive parents will have little to no training in parenting traumatized children. They do not understand what they're getting into. They don't think about this child having a life before coming to them, that this early life with the birth family is part of the child's story. They don't get that loss is inherent in adoption. The child has had to lose in order to gain. They don't know that adop-

tion feels like second-best to their children. Their first choice, generally, is to stay with their birth family. Parents don't get the help with their own losses and traumas, which impacts their parenting.

I'd say about 50 percent of adoptees are dealing with a "failure to launch," feeling as if they don't belong, and difficulties with relationships. This includes choosing friends who influence them toward negative and/or high-risk behavior.

Adoption itself is trauma, a loss. The past experiences of the child can be traumatic. The current living situation with the adoptive family can also be traumatic. It has less to do with the age and has more to do with the number of times the child was moved (pre-adoption) and the quality of each relationship.

———

Alicia Krpan is a licensed mental health counselor at Des Moines Pastoral Counseling Center in Des Moines, Iowa. She received her Master's Degree in Counseling Psychology from the University of Calgary in Canada. She provides counseling to children, adolescents, and adults with diverse emotional concerns. She has special interest in the areas of anxiety, attachment, life transitions, and trauma and is a trained clinician in EMDR (eye movement desensitization and reprocessing *to process strong feelings related to trauma*, mindfulness, and art- and play-based approaches).

Robin: *What have you found in your practice that ties all adoption stories together?*

Alicia: *Great intentions, love, and a desire to impact the children's lives in the case of pre-teen adoptions.*

Robin: *Of the clients you've worked with, approximately what percentage were adopted at birth versus adopted after the first year of life?*

Alicia: Of the clients I currently work with, *I'd say about 30 percent were adopted at birth, and 70 percent at seven to fourteen years of age. I don't have any clients between the ages of 1 and 7 right now.*

Robin: *What percentage of adoptees have intellectual knowledge that they're loved and are worthy of love and belonging but "feel" the opposite is true?*

Alicia: *I see adults and teens that are aware of how much they were loved growing up and the many ways the adoptive parents showed up for them. However, as you pointed out, a high percentage (80 percent) have verbalized a feeling of not belonging.*

The expressions range from "I never quite fit," to "I tried but did not feel like I belonged," and "I get mad at myself for being like that" to "I can enjoy parts of myself with them, but other parts I don't." This incongruence between knowing and feeling is not unique among adoptees.

We share wounds, and it is a lifelong journey to find congruency. However, what I found that helps are having enough emotional repairing experiences that solidify the "feel" part.

Parents will come up with creative ways to convey to their children the amazing gift they are to them, how much they appreciate their biological parents for the gift of life, or how much they've changed their world. Children understand this at an intellectual level. However, in therapy, they express a sense of sorrow as if they are stuck in a continuous cycle of grieving the "what ifs." They often idealize the biological parent.

Robin: *What are some reasons adoptees, or their parents, are seeking help from you?*

Alicia: *Developmental trauma can manifest in different ways. Behaviors like aggression, clinginess, self-injury, extreme jealousy with siblings, defiance, anxiety, and depression are all symptoms that make sense if viewed from trauma framework lenses. The chief complaint from parents is "I never know what's going on in his/her head," "It seems we aren't connecting," "He (or she) just will not talk with me," or "Her mood changes so quickly."*

Parents with experience are often caught off-guard as the expectations are for the youth to express love and affection in ways that make sense to them (the parents). When a child with attachment or developmental trauma gets triggered by the same expressions of love and care, it cre-

ates confusion and disappointment. Parents start doubting their parenting skills or even suitability to parent these children.

Robin: *Are there varying degrees of reactive attachment disorder? Have you worked with adoptees at birth with some degree of RAD?*

Alicia: *Yes. In my opinion, RAD presents as a spectrum because every individual with early traumatic experiences demonstrates the symptoms at different levels. The clinical description of RAD in* The Diagnostic and Statistical Manual of Mental Disorders, Fifth Edition *describes it as severe withdrawal, aggression, self-injury, and emotional detachment. Some individuals meet the criteria with the most severe presentation, usually abused and/or neglected children during their first five years of life. Even in this population, RAD only occurs in 10 percent [of the adoptee population.]*

Some clients have developed healthy coping skills, and I believe this has to do with early professional intervention and well-trained parents. These parents have checked their expectations and understand their roles. This "low" level of RAD is evidenced in therapy by symptoms of hypo-aroused states. The adults that I have seen that might fit the "low" level of RAD are intellectually aware that their need was regularly met by their caregivers and have experienced healthy interpersonal relationships. However, personal experiences can still disrupt their attachment system, especially after significant adverse experiences.

Robin: *What are the current ways of treating RAD?*

Alicia: *Because trauma and neglect are barriers to neurological, emotional, social, and cognitive development, therapies have had to develop integrative/holistic ways to treat the individual. EMDR (eye movement desensitization and reprocessing) is a therapy that supports the expansion of the window of tolerance to process strong feelings related to traumatic experiences without losing a sense of self.*

I'd like to add a note here that the "window of tolerance" she is referring to is an idea developed by Dan Siegel, a clinical professor of psychiatry at UCLA's School of Medicine that describes "the best state of 'arousal' or stimulation in which we can function and thrive in everyday life."

Play therapy is helpful in offering repair of emotional experiences in a non-threatening way. Polyvagal-informed interventions [based on the science of feeling safe] to nurture a sense of safety within the body and art techniques are also helpful. In some cases, parent-child intervention therapy is helpful in building connection and safety.

Robin: *What would you say has been the most helpful?*

Alicia: *I believe using every single opportunity in therapy and at home to provide an emotional repairing experience is very helpful. Parents and therapists working together, communicating effectively, will make a tremen-*

dous difference in the outcomes. Flexibility, education in trauma, self-compassion, and humor are great tools when things become challenging. Every individual will present a different level/severity of symptoms, and the key is to meet them where they are. Some clients will benefit from more cognitive-based therapies and others from more sensory-oriented experiences. The rupture occurred within a relationship, and the healing will occur in the same space.

Robin: *Has it been your experience that love conquers all?*

Alicia: *I validate and understand it. When I talk about emotional repairing experiences, I'm talking about specific repair that has left a child with a negative belief about themselves that has to be specifically targeted in therapy and at home. Together in therapy, the parents can identify their child's negative beliefs through their history, adoption agency, triggers, and coping mechanisms (behaviors). These negative beliefs range from "I'm not good enough," and "I am not safe" to "I'm worthless" or "I'm responsible for everything."*

I hope that we can come up with a specific need the child has and then provide a repairing experience—that with love and compassion, we will create the healing. Love is a part of the equation. However, education, compassion, humor, support, patience, and more patience are what will conquer all the initial heartache.

Robin: *What hope can you give adoptive parents who are discouraged with what they're experiencing?*

Alicia: *Be present and forgive your child before you react to their behavior. Healing will come, but probably not as quickly as you'd like. Check your expectations.*

Please find a support system, a safe space, to process what this work can and will trigger in you. Take care of yourself and let others care for you. Your job is to plant a seed. It will pay off. You must be open to the currency style or the way he/she will show it to you.

Robin: *Where can the adoptive parent go to get help in their area? Is there a national registry or list of therapists who work with adoption issues?*

Alicia: *I have a couple of therapists in town I call upon for consultations and refer clients. I'm not sure about there being a national registry.*

Robin: *What is missing in equipping future adoptive parents?*

Alicia: *For future adoptive parents, please read about different experiences with adoption, discuss this with the adoption agency, and consider the possibility for individual therapy before they arrive at your home. For parents that have already adopted, get group support and individual therapy for themselves so they can safely discuss and process issues that arise with adoption.*

Robin: *What percentage of adoptees are dealing with failure to launch, feeling they don't belong, having difficulties with relationships, or choosing friends who influence them toward negative/high risk behavior?*

Alicia: *I'd say the majority of the population I see struggle with a concept of belonging and worthiness.*

In addition to these professionals' offerings, I'd like to suggest reading *The Body Keeps Score* by Bessel van der Kolk. His work tells parents how children "remember" things that happened to them before they had use of language. I also like Brené Brown's newest book, *Atlas of the Heart*, for exploring emotions and naming feelings. We can all struggle to put a name to what we're feeling. An adoptee has many layers added to this struggle. Words are so powerful and must be attached to the emotion for greater understanding.

Lastly, a color wheel of emotions chart is helpful to name our feelings more accurately and aids in understanding and communication with others. These can be used with parents and adoptees of all ages. Color wheels of emotions can be found by googling "color wheel of emotions" where you can choose what's best for the ages of your children. Even young adults find this tool helpful if they have a difficult time articulating the way they feel. You can also get in touch with me via my website.

Chapter Nine

IS SELF-COMPASSION SELFISH?

Have you ever had these thoughts?

To "set an inviting table" for my kids, I think I need to be in a better frame of mind myself. With all the misgivings, fears, and frailties in my own life, I'm needing a little compassion. And frankly, I'm not feeling the love for myself that I wish was feeling.

I confess; I have lived right there for a pretty good chunk of time. As I explored these thoughts, I came to discover something powerful. It started with a question: How am I supposed to love me? This presented a bit of a dilemma. I know I'm not supposed to think of myself as overly important, but how do I develop enough confidence to do what I need to do? And what does *self-compassion* even mean?

For starters, what is your self-talk? What do you say to yourself when no one else is listening? Does it sound anything like this?

"You stupid idiot! What were you thinking?"

"What made you think you could be his parent? You don't know enough!"

"Could you have possibly screwed this kid up any worse?"

"You'll never be the kind of parent you should be. You've made too many mistakes."

"I hate who I've become!"

"You just keep on messing things up. You've ruined them!"

"They'd be better off if you just left."

"You're not worth the paper you signed when adopting."

"They don't love you. You always say the wrong thing."

"You're just one big mistake!"

"You're a horrible example of a good parent."

"How could anyone love you?"

Perhaps, in our secret hearts, we can admit we've said some of these things to ourselves. Even for a moment, maybe we've slipped into some thoughts along these lines. But what exactly are we saying?

Over the course of the last several years, I became acquainted with the work of Dr. Brené Brown. In fact, I trained at her organization to become a Certified Daring Way™ facilitator because her work on shame and resilience had such a personal impact on me. Since then, I've co-facilitated groups in various states on these topics and have loved watching participants get free of some things that previously held them bound.

As a well-known researcher, author, and presenter, Dr. Brown distinguishes between shame and guilt. She says shame is the belief that *I am bad*. Guilt is the belief that *I did something bad*. In other words, we may agree that something we said or did was not our best choice. We could learn from it and make corrections. Then we would experience guilt. Guilt is easier to deal with because it can be corrected by changing our decisions. In the words of Maya

Angelou, we learn better; we do better. But to say or believe we *are* bad—well, how can that be corrected? This is shame at its core. Shame is a difficult foe because it's insidious. It comes to us when we least expect it. It sneaks up on us at the most surprising times and ways. We can feel shame and not even recognize it. Sometimes, it takes others to help us know what we're up against.

In my certification process, I learned there are two remedies for shame. They are self-compassion and empathy. To learn more about this, listen to Dr. Brown's TEDx Talks on shame and vulnerability on YouTube. These two talks are among the five most-watched TED Talks of all time! They must resonate with a lot of people!

Let's first look at self-compassion. We've already looked at negative self-talk. For our purposes here, I'd like you to ask yourself, "Would I say anything like this [what I'm saying to myself] to a close friend?" If not, maybe we need to explore this. Most of us would put forth our best efforts for a friend, and our words would most definitely include kindness. We might approach them with the perspective that they are doing the best they can.

What if we turned that on ourselves? What if we could direct this same kindness toward our own hearts? What if we could give ourselves permission to know that *we* are doing the best we can? Would you like to try it now? What words can you say to your own heart that would elicit kindness and a feeling of support? Think of what you may say to that friend you love. Now say that to your own heart. It may feel foreign at first. It will, more than likely, take some practice. In fact, self-compassion is a practice. It's something we need to cultivate in our lives if we are to move forward with courage. Would you agree that parenting requires a healthy dose of courage? Let's start with self-compassion.

We've all heard the familiar "flight attendant speech" at the beginning of every plane trip. They tell us, in the event of an emergency, to put our own oxygen masks on first and then turn to our children and help them get theirs on. We all know that if the "thinking person" is down, then there's no hope for the little one who is looking to them for help.

What if *we* are being kind to ourselves, adopting the belief that we are doing the best we can? How might that change the way we extend kindness to our adoptees? What might they feel about the way we are now speaking to them or supporting them?

This new way of looking at ourselves can benefit our children at any age. If we are currently parenting young (under our own roof) children or if they are already grown and out from under our direction, our self-kindness will be apparent to them. It, somehow, gives them permission to be kind to themselves too. And when we are accepting of ourselves, we experience hospitality within ourselves. This hospitality invites others in. Hospitality creates a safe place for conversation and learning. It creates a feeling of openness, of safety.

When I was at my lowest, I ran across a tool of self-compassion. Because I'm a Certified Daring Way™ facilitator, I became acquainted with the work of Kristen Neff. Kristen has spent decades researching self-compassion. Browsing her website, I found an experiment I could try in the privacy of my room. It seemed a little silly to me at first, but I decided I had nothing to lose. Closing the door, I turned on the recording and followed her instruction to the letter. I was led through a series of thoughts I had about myself. I came to the part of the experiment that led me to give myself a hug and speak tenderly to myself as I would a cherished friend. There, alone in the quietness of my room, I told myself, "I love you. You're doing the best you can. You're working hard to listen and understand. You are a good parent. You have loved well." When I heard these things come out of my mouth, I began to cry. I realized I'd never said those things to myself before, despite them being true. I realized, in those moments, how starved I was for affirmation and understanding. And I could receive it from myself in those sacred moments. That's the day the practice of self-compassion was born in me. I realized it had been a missing piece—because of my belief that self-compassion was selfish. On this day, I could cast aside that belief in deference to the fact that I felt empowered by this new practice.

The second weapon for fighting shame is empathy. Dr. Brené Brown talks about this in her work, distinguishing that empathy is connecting with the feelings of others, not the event or circumstances. This powerful realization that we're not alone dissipates shame.

This is an active experience as well. Instead of looking inward, we reach out to those who love us and who have earned the right to hear our story. It is important that we don't say too much to the wrong person and then later bitterly regret what we shared and to whom we've shared it. We must look to those who have walked a distance with us on this road. We must determine if they have our best in mind and if they will share the good, the bad, and the ugly with us. More than likely, they will be vulnerable about their own lives. There will be a camaraderie built over time. Perhaps time is the first thing we should look for. How much time have we had to share life with this person? For instance, we may have known this one for most of our lives but have shared little along the way. Perhaps we have known the person for less time than others but have shared much already and feel comfortable with the friendship we've built. Each has the others' good in mind and is *for* the other.

Once you've located and determined this kind of person, reach out to them in moments of self-doubt or when you're experiencing shame. Sometimes, we all need reminders of who we are. And these people can remind us when we've forgotten.

I'm fortunate enough to have such a friend. Not long ago, I found myself in a deep funk over something precious to me. I was sinking into a quagmire of self-doubt and even self-loathing. I was saying things like, "I wish I would've done that better, but now it's too late . . . I don't know if I can recover." Being the astute friend she is, she sent me an email reminding me who I am. She said, "You are His (God's) beloved . . . sad, grieving, traumatized and dignified, beautiful. HIS . . . I have thought of you as a great example of love, passion, and commitment for so many years. Yes, there is pain, but it does not define you. I love you, friend."

For me, this reached in and pulled me out and onto level ground. I could think differently and realized, while reading her response, that I'd been in shame. Reaching out to her and letting her express empathy was almost an instant cure for what I was telling myself. Then I could employ self-compassion practice, but only after I recognized I had been in shame.

Who can you think of that could whisper empathic words into your ears? Might you be willing to risk vulnerability with those people? If you have nobody that comes to mind just now, perhaps you could work on cultivating and surrounding yourself with listening, caring people. When building a small network of people like this, one must dare to risk a little at a time. To risk nothing is to gain nothing.

My husband, Jon, has an illustration I've always loved. He says to ponder a brick wall. Notice that there are only a limited number of bricks surrounding any given brick. There's simply not enough surface area to have more than a few touching any one brick. Yet, with only a few solid connections (glued with mortar), a strong wall can be built. Mortar, if you will, is that sticky stuff (involving trust) of which loving relationships are made.

In this journey of parenting adoptees, we need to employ the practices of self-compassion and empathy. We desperately need them to hold our heads up and continue. We need them in our lives to know we are enough and we belong in this role. There is a place for us, and we are important.

Adoptive parents are the ones who listen to their children's concerns late at night when we'd rather be sleeping, the ones who think through ways they can succeed in life, and the ones who pay and pay over and over (because we want them to have the best). We are parents at heart, in practice, and in our willingness to lay down our lives for our children.

As important as it is for adoptive parents to be kind to themselves, it is equally important for birth moms to "let themselves off the hook." Birth moms need to learn self-compassion, too. There are always circumstances that lead to these life-altering decisions. Even as they come to clarity on placement decisions, they must continue to deal with their feelings for years afterward. I hope to relay a few of their stories to give insight to adoptive parents. In my interviews with birth moms over the months, I have sat with them in compassion and gained a deep appreciation for their courageous decisions.

Recently, I spoke with a birth mom named Sandra. Now in her thirties, she was willing to sit down and give me her story.

> *I was nineteen years old, walking the streets with my young child when Bev found me. I was pregnant with my second child. I had no hope and no place to land. She helped me get off the street and figure out my next steps. CPS [Child Protective Services] got involved too.*

When my second child was born, I placed both of my children with a loving family to raise them in a good home. I wanted them to have a Christian upbringing and be cared for better than what I could give them.

Soon, I became pregnant again, and I wanted to try to parent my child this time. I realized when the child was four months old, I couldn't do it. I had no resources. I placed this child with the family that [was raising] my first two children.

My fourth pregnancy resulted from a rape. By this time, I was twenty-six years old and decided to place this baby with a family as well. I wanted my children to stay together if possible. I wanted them to have a relationship. The couple who was raising my first three already had a full house. I placed this fourth child with another family. It turned out the parents live close to each other and already knew each other.

After I placed my children, I went back to school and got a degree. I eventually got married. I haven't had any more children. I do have dreams for me to see my children grow up, be happy, and have what I didn't have as a child or teenager.

All my adoptions are open adoptions. I speak to my adoptive moms regularly via phone and [social] media. I don't see the kids, but I have gotten to see pictures of them on Facebook. I have a good relationship with all my adoptive moms. I write letters and send them to the kids.

I want to meet the kids when they're ready. I don't want to push myself on them if they're not ready. I'd love to have a relationship with them when they want it. I'd like to tell them that I couldn't take care of them. I'd love to know they're doing okay in their lives and for them to know that I did this because I love them.

I'd like to write a letter and just hand it to them. I'd tell the adoptive mom how much I appreciate her for taking on my three children. I chose the adoptive parent profile based on what they said, their story. What I loved about the family was how much the dad loved the mom and the kids. I loved how she [the adoptive mom] had a caring spirit. She even called during my second pregnancy just to check up on me.

———————

Michelle tells her story of placing her child for adoption.

Right out of high school, I was living with my boyfriend and got pregnant with twins. He wanted nothing to do with the whole thing. When that relationship didn't work out, I found my way to a group home for those with unplanned pregnancies. I was about six months along. They taught us about what it was like to parent and gave us a real view of what we would be facing ahead. They also taught us life skills and brought up the option of adoption. I felt they were truly helping me without any pressure to make a certain choice.

My own home life had been less than good, and I had planned to learn everything I could about parenting throughout the rest of my pregnancy so I could do better than what I had. But as I stayed at the home, I met a girl who was planning to place her child in a married couple's home once she delivered. I had never thought about it. I watched her choose her couple and talked with her about it. I faced the very hard truth that I couldn't give my babies what I wanted them to have. I wanted them to have stability; I wanted them to have a home with united parents. I wanted them to go to college, play sports, and never have to worry or wonder if they were loved. And I didn't want to be my mother.

It just became clear that I needed to place [my kids] in a loving home. As gut-wrenching as it was, it was the best choice for my babies to get what they deserved. I was handed five photo albums to look through to consider which set of parents would be best for my babies. When I got to number three, I knew immediately. The thing that got me was the way he was looking at her. It was a candid shot of them together. I wanted that kind of dad for them. He was so loving. There was truth, vulnerability, love, and compassion in this couple. One month after choosing them, we got to meet face to face. They were just as I imagined.

I had my sonogram with me and waited to talk with them a bit before showing them. At that time, they thought it was a single child. When I showed them the picture, they cried because they had wanted twins. There were many confirmations like this for me throughout the process.

As much as I was comfortable with them, placing my twins for adoption became very difficult. In fact, after I gave birth, I took my babies home with me for six days. I wanted to feel their skin, make an imprint in their minds, smell their milk breath, and just be with them. I almost turned back from adoption because I just didn't think I could go through with it. But as I thought it through, again and again, I knew it was best for them and released them for adoption at the end of the six days. I felt so guilty. I was devastated. I kept hearing the words of others saying, "How could you do that?" and was so heartbroken. People around me would say things like, "You need to face your problem. It's your responsibility" and "You're just taking the easy way out." Anybody who's had to make this kind of decision knows it's anything but easy. I did it out of love! During the days that preceded and followed placement, I was somewhat comforted with church, prayer, and counseling. In fact, the people at the group home were so supportive. I had nobody else.

I had a hard time after that—for a couple of years. I kind of dropped out and was very depressed. A lot of those days have been blocked from my mind, I think. I moved around and lived with one friend and then another. I got pregnant again by another guy who didn't work out. And I chose to keep and parent [that child]. Because placing was so hard on me, I just couldn't do it again.

The adoptive parents were good to me in that they sent pictures and wrote letters about how the twins were growing. Once, they sent a hand-written note by each of the kids to me so I would have something in their own handwriting. I still have those letters.

In the years that followed, I opened a home daycare for infants up to twelve months old and got to watch many take their first steps, roll over for the first time, and say their first words. All the things I missed with my twins, I got to have with others. I was careful to document these things and give them to the parents.

If I got to meet the adoptive mom again, I'd hug her neck. I'd thank her and tell her she's amazing. I'd want to hear all about their growing-up years . . . their hardships and their joys.

If I had the chance to meet the twins, I would love to tell them I love them and that's why I did it. It wasn't about me. I would hope they could say to me that they're glad and have had a wonderful life. I'd love to know they have Jesus at the center of their lives, that they've had stability and have never wondered if they're loved. I would love for them to say they'd keep in touch in whatever way was best for them. I'd love to see them and for them to meet their half-sibling. I guess I still need affirmation about my decision, even after all these years. I was eighteen then, and now I'm forty-two.

When asked what she's been able to do with her life since placing her twins for adoption, Michelle told me she never went to college but has co-owned a feed store with her husband and is a veterinary assistant working on her licensure to be a veterinary technician.

———————

Mary, now in her fifties, shares her story from despair to redemption.

> *At forty-two years old, I was in a bad marriage and miserable. I was working for my husband, at this time, and this involved some traveling. While traveling in a different state, I was asked to go check on a friend of his because he was going through a divorce. This man and I met for dinner. He offered to buy me a drink. He saw I was miserable and asked me about it. I was surprised that he noticed my unhappiness. I had tried so hard to make this marriage work and be a loving wife. When he offered me that drink, I let anger get the best of me. After the first drink, I had several more. I put myself in a situation where I blacked out and didn't recall the rest of that evening. That choice changed my life forever.*
>
> *I'd always been told by several doctors that I would never be able to become pregnant. Imagine my shock when I found out I was! I was devastated because I was married to someone else, and we hadn't been in a good place for some time. There had been no physical contact, so there was no hiding this.*

Shortly, I lost my marriage, my friends, and a place to live. My job was gone too. I found myself all alone in the world with no place to go. I was completely lost, even suicidal. I reached out to a friend of mine who lived across the ocean in the Middle East. I was considering an abortion because I just had no resources. This friend told me that the life inside my body was a miracle, and I should respect the life that was inside. She found a pregnancy resource center (PRC) near me and told me to go there.

I showed up at the PRC and was met with such love and support. I couldn't believe it. They sent me to get a sonogram, and I found out I was five weeks pregnant. These people, too, acknowledged what a miracle this child was and told me to honor the life within me. The doctor showed me the baby's heartbeat, and I was able to hear it. That's when I heard in my heart these words: "Mary, I have a special purpose for this child." I felt this was God saying this to my heart. I said, "I will do whatever You tell me to do." I never thought about abortion again. I would carry this child to term. I would be a parent if that was best, but I wanted the very best for this child, whatever that meant.

My family of origin hadn't been good, and I had so many gaps. Whatever gender this child would be, I realized I would not be parenting them. My plan was to carry the child to term, place them for adoption, and then just die. I felt I couldn't face the choices I'd made and how they had changed my life. I couldn't see how I could ever feel better or be better than this decision, which brought me to pregnancy. I had made such a mess of my life and others' lives.

I was able to stay with my friend's mom for a short time. Through a series of friendships, my situation was made clear to the director of a small home for women with unplanned pregnancies. This amazing woman opened the doors for me, and I lived there for the remainder of my pregnancy. I was so loved and supported in ways I'd never experienced before. There was no judgment. There were resources made available to me, even though I was forty-two years old. The staff there helped me so much. I thought there might be a purpose for my life too.

I'd planned to place this child in someone else's home. I began looking at "Life Books." These were a type of portfolio with a couple's story and pictures so I could get to know them a little before choosing to meet them. I quickly landed on a certain couple based on the way they related to their parents, extended family, and each other. They were older, and I liked that. I noticed we had many of the same interests, and they just seemed to take a similar approach to life as me.

We met in person with a supervisor from the unplanned pregnancy home. This couple was as I had imagined. I just loved them. When they left, I wondered if I'd ever see them again. I tried not to have any expectations.

To my delight, the woman, Kate, started writing me letters. It was great to hear from her. Throughout the rest of my pregnancy, we exchanged letters and even some pictures. Trust was being built, and I was so sure of my decision to place with Kate and Robert. Simultaneously, my soul was being healed too. I wasn't sure how, but I felt like there would be a life for me after my pregnancy.

At age forty-two, I delivered my child, Ella. Kate and Robert were in constant communication with the supervisor of the home. They were kept abreast of how I was doing and then were told I had delivered a baby girl. I stayed in the hospital for three days and got to spend time with Ella. Shortly thereafter, it was "Placement Day." That day was so special. I handed my little Ella over to them, knowing I'd made the right choice.

I wasn't expecting to feel the extreme grief and depression that came. And so many tears! The supervisor and director of the home I'd been living in walked me through those difficult days that followed. Intellectually, I knew I'd made the right choice, but the emotional upheaval within me was a different thing altogether. I was grieving, and it was very real.

Kate and I continued exchanging letters and pictures, along with updates on Ella's progression. More trust was being established between us. I was always so grateful to Ella's parents because they were doing such a fabulous job with her. I expressed this gratitude, as well. Kate and I were becoming friends. I think this happened due to us both being more mature, confident, and secure about this decision. We knew it was best for Ella. We began texting each other and keeping in touch. We would meet once a year at a neutral location. When Ella was four years old, Kate and Robert invited me to their house. We have been continuing this yearly tradition since.

Ella knew me first as her "Tummy Mommy." Now, she calls me Miss Mary. I love watching her grow and knowing she's in the exact perfect place for her to have her best life. She is being educated, and she enjoys a big extended family, which is something I could never have given her. She is being raised in a loving, secure home and has confidence. She knows we all love her, and this is the best for her. She's flourishing! And that's what I want for her.

I feel God has been with me too. I live and work in a different state but get to see her grow through pictures and hear the updates from Kate. We even have some Zoom calls every so often.

I work two jobs to make my bills because one of my jobs doesn't pay much. But I get to invest in others by doing this job, and I like that. If I was raising Ella, we would be struggling. I would probably have to work four jobs if I were parenting. By not parenting, we both are doing well. In addition, I have more time to pursue friendships, and I love volunteering. If I was a single parent, I couldn't do any of these types of things because I wouldn't have the time or money. So I can see the bigger picture now, as it relates to my decision to place Ella. I, too, have a life, just like I envisioned when hope was beginning to rise in me, those many years ago.

The thing that means a lot to me is trying to be the best support to Kate and Robert as they raise Ella and her sibling. I offer to get a hotel on those yearly visits I make. They tell me to stay with them, but I'm always open to this if things change. Whatever's best for Ella is what I want. I feel we are working as a unit to support Ella in her life. It makes me happy to know that Ella is stable and growing up in such a wonderful family. I call them my "forever family." They hold such a special place in my heart. Ella is now almost nine years old, and I am very confident that I made a great decision to place her with Kate and Robert.

I'd like to tell everybody how wonderful adoption is. I'd like to say that if you can give a child the greatest life, and it's through adoption, don't be afraid. God will bless you and your child abundantly—in ways you can't imagine!

———

I met Lulu over thirty years ago. Now in her fifties, she generously tells her story.

I grew up with a warped definition of love. Love, in my experience, did not set boundaries, and love and shame were often intertwined. Although I now cringe at even seeing the words on paper, my pregnancy resulted from having an affair with a much older married man. I thought I loved him, but in fact, we barely knew each other, and we had no meaningful conversation that I can recall.

When I told Rod that I was pregnant, he tried everything in his playbook to get me to abort the pregnancy. He tried kindness, anger, and self-pity. He was frightened, and I understood that. He had a wife and a young son at home, and he was supporting other children from his first wife. But I wouldn't entertain the idea of abortion. I wanted my baby, although I had no intention of upending his life by requiring him to help me. We broke off the relationship immediately.

I was living with my mother and stepfather at the time and didn't have any other place to go. My mother and sister encouraged me to give the baby up for adoption, but I was quietly resistant and tried to find a way to keep her. When my mother told me several weeks into my pregnancy that she and my stepfather could not help me if I decided to raise the child, I couldn't find a way through. I tried for weeks to picture a good life for this baby and me, and as much as I wanted that, I couldn't see it.

I considered adoption, and it seemed increasingly like the best option. If I remember correctly, as this was many years ago, I was about six months pregnant when I finally made the unequivocal decision to place my child. The moment came when I was approached by a couple who were close friends of mine. They told me they had friends who had a four-year-old adopted son, and they were looking to adopt again. I believe I decided then and there, as they told me about the couple, that they were the ones I wanted to be the parents of my baby. There were four reasons I chose them. One, I had tremendous respect for my friends who recommended them. I felt confident they were good people and would provide a good home. Second, I liked the idea of my child having an older brother who was also adopted. Third, at that time, it was very important to me that she grow up in a Christian home. Fourth, I wanted my baby to have a mother who could stay home with her. I knew that if Alexandra were anything like me, she would thrive in that environment. And she certainly did.

My greatest hope for Alexandra was that she would grow up healthy and happy. I also hoped that she would be afforded all the opportunities she would need to chart her course and fulfill her hopes for herself.

Although I desperately wanted to raise her, I knew that giving her up to a loving, nurturing family would give her the best chance at a good life. My life would have looked so very different if I had not made that choice. Because I did not raise her, I focused on improving my own trajectory. I had always been a weak student, and I had very little respect for myself, but I decided to go to college full time. I surprised myself by not only being able to keep up but by finding that I have a genuine love of learning. In a meandering sort of way, I eventually earned a clinical doctorate and cannot imagine a career I would have enjoyed more than the one I am in. Alexandra was the impetus for me going to school. Although I will always have an abiding sadness at not having had any children of my own, I met a wonderfully supportive man and married into grandmotherhood. I have been rewarded beyond measure in that role. I have also found fulfillment in who I have become and in how I give back through my work.

When Alexandra was twenty-three, I met her. She was about the same age as I was when she was born. I now have a relationship with her that I cherish. Our time together is comfortable and involves a lot of laughter. I would like to spend more time with her, perhaps seeing her a few times a year, but I let Alexandra set the tone for our relationship, and that is as it should be. For me, it feels a little like wanting a big slice of chocolate cake and only being given a bite. I loved that one bite but long for the next one.

Alexandra had a much healthier upbringing than I did. I wanted her to be raised in a Christian family, and she grew to be a beautiful, strong Christian lady. I, on the other hand, no longer hold those same beliefs, and that has created something of a divide between us.

I had the opportunity to speak with Alexandra's mother several years ago. I carefully planned what I was going to say and then, of course, I blubbered through the whole conversation. I made a real mess of it. Essentially, I told her how happy I was that Alexandra had the life that I so wanted her to have and would never have been able to give her. I thanked her for making that possible.

These birth moms were so generous in telling their stories to me. I sat with them and their experiences in empathy. I hope you can see this side of the triad too. It doesn't matter if your adoption is open, closed, or a hybrid of these. Understanding the birth mom's perspective is important. Walking in another (wo)man's shoes gives the needed perspective for the entire journey. It can be a very diffusing piece of insight. For me, it was a camping ground for compassion and self-compassion. And that's a very good thing!

Chapter Ten

COMMUNITY IS A SUPERPOWER

While my interviews are certainly not exhaustive, there have been many. I want to share with you some stories that have impacted me. They have led me to discover just how important it is to surround the adoptive family with others who are also raising adoptees. If an adoptive parent feels there are no differences between adoptees and biological children, they may miss this very important messaging. From where I stand now, I see this as something we missed while raising our children.

Carrie and Kyle have been friends of ours since before they married. After a few years of marriage, they found out they couldn't have children, so they considered adoption. Theirs was a long and winding road, but they eventually found an agency and started the process to adopt. Here is their story.

> *As a twenty-year-old, I was told I'd probably not be able to bear children. Once Kyle and I began dating seri-*

ously, we talked about infertility and both agreed we'd just adopt. After we married, we waited the obligatory three years before any agency would consider us. It was important to us to find an agency that supported the birth mother as much as they did us. Because of my close relationship with a friend who'd placed a baby for adoption, I knew the importance of that support. I never forgot how she felt and the support she did not *receive while pregnant—as well as after she placed her child. I came to believe that agencies should give equal weight to all three parts of the adoption triad.*

I was twenty-nine years old when our first daughter came to us at birth. We would adopt two more children. When our first child was four years old, she asked about her birth mom, saying, "Do you think she misses me?" I assured her she did. Shortly afterward, we met her birth mom. Our daughter went right up to her and said, "My mama said I grew in your tummy." Her birth mom confirmed that to her.

When our daughter was around eight or nine years old, she asked me if I wished she'd grown in my tummy. I told her no; if she'd grown in my tummy, she wouldn't be her, and I wouldn't change a thing about her.

As our children grew, we brought attention to their genetics, their physical similarities to their birth mothers, their characteristics, and more. We showed the kids pictures about twice a year. Whenever it was pertinent, we openly talked about adoption and their birth mothers.

When one of our daughters began fantastical thinking about her birth mom, I got out the picture again and rehearsed the fact that she grew in this woman's tummy. It was as though she'd forgotten. After seeing the picture, she quit fantasizing and realized she was just a normal woman, not a princess like she'd dreamed up.

Our agency provided a lot of training to adoptive parents. While waiting for our placement, we went through training in groups with other prospective adoptive parents. We met monthly and became quite close to these folks. The agency also offered other adoptive parent groups and even mentors, if desired. After we adopted our children, these groups continued to meet twice a year for ten years! There were probably about thirty couples in total. So our kids grew up with adoptive families all their lives. Besides friends who had biological children, they were around many who were adopted. Adoption never seemed odd to them.

Our relationship with each of our children is very close. They each call us every day. Though they don't live with us now, they are well-connected. One of them is married. Another one is [single]. And then there's another who is unmarried and a new mom. While we don't always approve of their lifestyles, we have always valued the relationship more.

When our oldest got married, she invited her birth mom. I was okay with this until she became a focal point at the wedding. I didn't resent her being there. I just felt I didn't like sharing this with her because it was ours to enjoy, but I had to share that day. I felt (and still do) the invisible string attached to my heart and connected to the birth mom. Every now and again, that string gets tugged a little.

When our kids were teenagers, there was the normal angst. Some of them kept secrets and went with boys we didn't approve of. I never felt this was directly tied to being adopted, rather just trying their hand at independence. I think I had a facedown time when one of our children ran away from home to be with one such boy. I was hurt, mad, and disappointed and took it personally. She wasn't following the script I'd written for her life.

You asked me how I felt I did as a parent. It depends on the day you ask—ha-ha. I can say I did the best I could with the information I had at the time. One of our kids has ADHD, and I just didn't see it. I was hard on this one. I couldn't understand why directions just couldn't be followed. The other kids followed instructions, but this one just wouldn't. I took it for disobedience and now wish I'd known so I could get treatment. Once I became aware, I got support, and medication helped them order thoughts and behavior followed. My intentions were always good. I was too hard on this one. I apologized to this child later as an adult and was given a full pardon, but I just wish I could've done better earlier. Impulse control just wasn't there, and I was late in coming to grips with why. Other parents would tell me I did a good job raising my kids.

The way we prepared for adoption was to read books on the subject. And the other adoptive families that were always part of our lives served to normalize everything. If I had a question about anything I was seeing, I'd ask other adoptive moms to get a better understanding. I feel that helped so much. I never went without resources. It was all along the way while raising them. I would just avail myself of things that came along. Movies, other stories of adoption, etc. . . . we would just bring that into our world. And our kids followed suit.

Our relationship with each one of our children is very close. I'd say when they were young, one of them gravitated more to Kyle than me. That was the one I was so hard on and didn't understand at the time. But now, all of them are close to us both.

The thing I regret now is not keeping up with the birth moms. I wish I'd been more consistent with them. I feel pretty good at this point . . . no real regrets about open adoption.

One thing I'd like to say before we leave. I worked, for some time, with adoptive parents in the adoption agency we used. The thing I noticed was this: those who struggled for years with infertility as their big obstacle and finally came to the choice of adoption versus the ones who moved quickly from infertility to adoption seemed to struggle much more with the entire process. I believe they carried grief into adoption that lingered and made it harder for them. Their expectations were very high. I believe that their injury was so much deeper when things didn't go as expected.

In talking with this next adoptive mom, I found another similarity in how she and her husband raised their adoptive children. I've known Betty for about ten years. This is Betty's story:

We wanted to build our family through both birth and adoption. We thought it would be a grand adventure and dreamed that our biological children would get along well with our adopted children, and we would be a multiracial family.

Our adopted daughter came to us at ten months old from India. She had been moved around four to five times before she came to us. She had a much harder time adapting than our adopted son, who was also from India. It was important to our daughter that there be someone else who looked like her. That was, in part, why we adopted again from India. She once said, "Our family is just right. We have two brown, two white, two boys, and two girls."

Right away, we noticed things about her. For instance, she destroyed our son's Lego castles and took apart his jigsaw puzzles. She refused any physical contact with her father for the first several years. A few years passed, and more behaviors began to show up. She screamed at the top of her lungs for two minutes straight.

I was already working in the field of adoption as a case-worker, so I thought I was well-prepared. However, it's very different to live with an unattached child than it is to be in the social worker role.

Along the way, we've gotten our kids therapy. There have also been ten surgeries for things like cleft lip and palate, nose revisions, ear tubes, and dental implants. Of course, prayer has been a very present part of our help.

We've had our share of ups and downs. At this point, our kids are all young adults, and we're okay. It was tough when all four of them were young and at home. Having other adoptive parents as friends helped so much. These friends don't judge. I can't say enough about that. I'd say having other adoptive families to do life with is the one thing that's helped the most.

Our comfort in those days was found in God. Our faith . . . knowing God was with us helped tremendously.

I guess one trial that brought me down was when our birth daughter hit our adopted son in the mall one day. A woman saw this and called the police saying our daughter was assaulting "this poor foster child." The police came and interviewed me.

Our adopted daughter is doing well now, at age thirty. Our adopted son has graduated from college and is trying to find his way as an adult.

Besides walking alongside other adoptive families, the things that have been effective are choosing to live near the Indian sector of our town, traveling to India with all our children, trying (albeit unsuccessfully) to locate our daughter's birth family, visiting our children's foster family and orphanage, and talking to all our kids about adoption-related topics.

In speaking with these two moms, I found them to be largely satisfied with the way their adoptees are growing and the way their families relate to one another. They, for the most part, are joyful and positive about adoption, and both were surrounded by adoptive families while they were raising their children. I consider this knowledge to be a gift.

To say there are no differences between adoptees and biological children is to undermine the help we might receive. The old saying, "it takes a village" is certainly true through this lens. When we adoptive parents avail ourselves of other adoptive families, we normalize adoption for our kids, we get the nonjudgmental support we need in difficult times, and we experience the joy of watching other adoptees and their parents grow as we contribute to them. As stated above, lifelong friendships have been created too. It takes the "I'm all alone in this" out of the equation, and the pain we shoulder is shared by others who care.

My friend Cathy, a single mom, is currently raising an adoptee. I asked her recently to share some thoughts about raising her child around other adoptive families. Below are her words.

In answer to your question, Melody has grown up with tons of adopted children, families, and a birth parent. She has friends who were adopted cross-racially. She sees adoption as a normal part of life. She knows birth parents and their unselfish love for their children they are placing for adoption and has witnessed the grief they experience. It helps her understand better the love her birth parents have for her. She has gone through ministry with me and seen the journey kids take through their adoption experience. She sees older kiddos go from trauma to stability. It has made her a more compassionate person.

If you look up and wonder, "Why do I feel so alone in this?" please consider finding a network of people to walk alongside in this life. It's so important to find at least *some* who are also raising adoptees. There are differences that the biological parent just won't be able to understand (unless they've adopted too). It won't be for their lack of love and interest in you. It's just that they may not understand the rejection that drives adoptees.

Sometimes, we find grandparents stuck in some ways of thinking that limit their ability to be supportive. Heck, many of us adoptive parents don't understand it. This is even more reason to put yourself in a community of others who are also making mistakes but seeking to grow. I can suggest looking for those who are kind and forgiving of themselves and others. Look for people who want to learn and do better. Being vulnerable with others, in the right setting, can promote connection and, sometimes, a lifelong relationship.

I met my friend, Liddy, about fifteen years ago. She and her husband, Ivan, adopted three kids with special needs who were older when they came into their home. I was privileged to observe Liddy as she educated them at home, spoke tenderly to them, and gave copious amounts of time and resources, tending to the needs of each of their children. She and her husband went to great lengths to give their kids all of the help they needed. When they reached young adulthood, a couple of them made choices to pull away from Liddy and Ivan and the values they had been taught. While this is not what they had hoped for, they've remained committed to fulfilling their parental roles as the journey unfolds. Now, Liddy's comments are, "Who knew there was so much to parenting? What a ride!"

Liddy knew another adoptive mom across town. This mom had problems of her own. Because of their friendship, they began talking more often about all things concerning adoption. They realized they could benefit from meeting together regularly. In implementing this practice, they began hearing of other adoptive moms who needed such support in their adoption journeys. At first, they huddled in each other's homes. They met at parks and other places. As the group grew into what is now a good-sized group, they settled on meeting in a church. New adoptive moms are still hearing of this group and coming from miles away just for the encouragement. The older, more experienced moms listen and support the newer adoptive moms. In giving to these young adoptive moms, Liddy and her friend have found solace. Liddy told me recently that she wished she'd had support like this while she was raising her children but is now trying to give to others what she didn't have. I say, *God bless Liddy!* What a gift to extend to others while our own hearts are coming to terms.

I told Liddy in our recent conversation that my definition of success has changed. Earlier in life, as a new adoptive mom, I had such high expectations of myself and my children. I pushed them to be all they could be. At this point in my life, I think I pushed them too hard. I pushed myself too.

I have come to grips with the fact that my children and I have different DNA, different ways of doing things, different expectations for our own lives, and different outcomes as well. No matter what they choose to do with their lives, I have done my best with the knowledge and strength afforded me at the time. Through that lens, I can say I have been a successful parent. I can say that while knowing full well I was (and am still) imperfect. I made tons of mistakes. And so have my kids. But regardless of their choices, I can stand in the light of what I've done as their parent. A big reason I have come to this way of thinking is that I now have a community of understanding parents alongside me.

One way of acquiring your group of sojourners might be to look up adoption groups on the internet. Maybe there is one near you. I recently googled "adoptive parent support groups" in a particular state. I found several regions, cities, and zip codes that offered groups. You could also contact a church and ask if there is such a group. There may be a resource like this at a nearby college or even a civic organization. And don't forget the crisis pregnancy centers in your area. Many of these are venturing out in broader ways to accommodate the needs of the whole adoption triad. It is my sincere hope you can find a group of others who are walking through adoption. There's such power in connection. I dare say you have a lot to give as well as receive. May your search be fruitful.

Chapter Eleven

WHO'S LIVING IN MY HOUSE?

I recently interviewed an adult adoptee who was from a different country than her adoptive parents. Both parents and the child needed to learn the other's language to communicate. I pondered this feat and thought they were super courageous in undertaking this task. But, of course, it's necessary.

And then I had a thought, "Actually, every adoptive parent and child must undertake this task." We, as adoptive parents, must learn our children's "language." We must study them, noticing how they best learn and grasp concepts. This is what I call "unwrapping our gifts." When we first receive these gifts in our home and care, we don't know them at all. We must get to know them. What are their personalities? What will emerge? What will their values be? We know this will take a lot more time than unwrapping a boxed gift. It may take a lifetime. But I believe it will be worth the effort.

We know that no two people are identical. Each of us is hard-wired a little differently. In this book, we've discussed some various issues that have surfaced with the adoptee. There are different things that come up when raising an adoptee who's come from another country with cultures to consider. Different issues can emerge with adoptees who have a different skin color than the adoptive parent. There are the obvious issues, ones that accompany developmental delays or other mental health challenges. And there are things that come into play when there's been drug/alcohol abuse and other kinds of abuse or neglect while in the womb or outside of the womb. How in the world can we know who these little ones are and what they need? How might understanding personalities within each of these situations help?

When our girls were young, we came upon a precious little book, *The Treasure Tree* by Trent and Smalley. A friend gifted us with this beautifully illustrated children's book, which educated readers on the four basic temperament types. Our girls were having a difficult time getting along. This little treasure helped soothe feelings and grant understanding of ways we are different and the specialness of each one. They automatically pointed out themselves and each other in the characters as we read along. They even had a few things to say about us. After reading this book together, there was more peace in our home. We would draw attention to the fact that each one was demonstrating their personality type in a certain instance and note the value of each other. We needed each other because of our differences, not because of our similarities. I can highly recommend this book to any parent with elementary-age children.

Of course, if your children are older, you can have them take a personality test. We had our girls do this when they were teenagers, and they seemed to enjoy learning more about themselves and each other, as well as their parents. Popular tests include the

Disc Assessment and The Big Five, outlining a person's openness, conscientiousness, extroversion, agreeableness, and neuroticism.

Another way to better understand personalities is the popular Myers-Briggs test. Many businesses offer this in their training departments as a way of affording a greater understanding of who is at the table. One of their end goals may be to help people get along with each other. It is remarkable what can come from knowing ourselves and others. I would like to say here that it is tempting to disparage others for who they are or how they act at any given moment. This is not the goal of taking personality tests. We each have "negative" default actions as well as "positive" ones. No one person has all the "good" traits or all the "bad" traits. We are all a mixed bag of both. When we seek to understand, instead of achieving superiority, we are all better served.

Recently, I was introduced to the Enneagram. I have found this tool to be quite helpful in understanding myself and others. In short, it's a personality *description* based on nine numbers, which highlight unique characteristics according to each number. The diagram used to teach this looks like a clock or star with the number 9 at the top, followed by a 1 just to the right of the 9. The numbers go in a clockwise motion.

Suzanne Stabile is a leading expert in training others in the Enneagram. A person's Enneagram number is determined, according to Stabile, by their genetic predisposition. As I understand it, our numbers are indicators of our motivations and we retain this indicator throughout our lives. We move across healthy, average, excess, or unhealthy in our number at any given time. Some may even move to a more pathological stance for reasons we won't discuss here. See the Additional Resources page for more details on any of these assessments.

A few months ago, I listened to a podcast called "Trauma and Adoption: The Enneagram Journey." The main speakers were Suzanne Stabile, an adult adoptee and an Enneagram specialist, and Dr. Barbara Rila, a psychologist specializing in treating children with trauma. They agreed on a definition of trauma as "something that threatens or feels as if it threatens our survival, be it physical, emotional, and/or spiritual."

This three-part podcast was so interesting to me that I booked a flight across the country to attend a conference on the subject taught by Suzanne Stabile. She's been working with the Enneagram for decades. To prepare for the conference, I also read the book, *The Road Back to You* by Ian Morgan Cron and Suzanne Stabile. I would like to recommend this book to you if you are interested in understanding the Enneagram.

I was not disappointed. I sat with about 150 others who had come in from all over the USA. With pen and paper in hand, I sought to capture everything. It was like drinking from a firehose. Knowledge just poured out of her. At times, we all found ourselves in tears over what we were learning. Like all meaningful knowledge, it made me take a step back to look at how I had raised our beauties. I recoiled and thought, "If only I had known!" I fought to stay present with her continual plethora of ongoing information. But I couldn't help, once again, from feeling like a failure.

As I seek to bring hope to you, I want to be transparent because I am still learning and growing right along with you. It appears to be a lifelong journey of learning, accepting, forgiving (myself and my children), and releasing. And that, my friend, is the crux of being a parent. With adoption, however, we, as parents, must seek to understand our children (even adult children) as they are. They come from other DNA. Since the mirroring that biological parents and children enjoy is missing, adoptive parents must work a little harder at unwrapping the gifts we've been given.

Although there are many personality tests, as evidenced by googling online, I have found the Enneagram sheds a lot of light on so much in my life, family, and friends. I've been sitting with this since I returned from that workshop I mentioned. I've asked myself, "Do I really love people for how God made them, or am I wishing they were more like me?" A tough question, and perhaps you've thought the same thing.

Below, I will try to give an extremely brief synopsis of the different number types based on my reading and gleaning from Suzanne's extensive work on the subject. I hope you will learn about it in more depth. A good place to start would be to read anything by Suzanne Stabile.

When I was taught the Enneagram, the teacher began with the number 9 on the diagram, so I will repeat her lead here. I learned I am a 9, and as a 9, I dislike confrontation. I would rather have root canals than confront someone—or even be in the same room with confrontation. By nature, I am a peace-lover. My happy place is being surrounded by peaceful relationships, nature, or soft, word-less music. I am a peacemaker, if you will. Now that sounds great, except that peacemakers tend to find themselves in places that need peace to be made. Isn't that fun? Now, in parenting, I want my children to just "get it" without me having to intervene or confront the behavior. I want them to love peace as much as I do. I might let a lot go by that needs my attention and intervention.

A Type 9 can understand both sides of an argument and can affirm both sides for what they are saying. Nines are infamous for procrastination and indecision.

A Type 9 can benefit from a loving parent looking at them and saying, "I want to hear your opinion about . . ." A 9 often gets swept along because they are so agreeable. Sometimes, this translates to "It doesn't matter what I think or see," so they become accustomed to being invisible. Being asked their opinion can help a 9 see they are valued as well as help them develop their voice.

A Type 1 personality tries very hard to get things "right." They are hard on themselves, as well as others. It's all an attempt at being the best they can be. Many times, this translates to, "It must be perfect." Naturally, perfection is an elusive goal. A type 1 feels frustrated and works all the harder. The rest of us need 1s to raise our games and inspire us to live closer to our potential.

It is important for a parent of a Type 1 to affirm their child for *who* they are. The effort is the desired outcome, not perfection. How can a parent lovingly encourage their Type 1 while teaching them there are other acceptable ways of doing things?

A Type 1 friend recently reported, "I think I would've benefited from hearing, 'You're enjoyable, delightful, and appreciated for what you bring to the table even among the imperfections.' I needed to know I was good enough."

Another Type 1 reported it would've helped to hear, "We support you and trust you. Even though your journey may be different from ours was, or how we think (or want) yours to be, that is okay.' I think it may have relieved some of the pressure I felt to be the 'perfect child,' who felt like sometimes support depended on how well I was doing and made me think with a very performance-based motivation."

A Type 2 personality is very "others focused." Twos can feel other people's emotions better than they can identify with their own. They need to be needed and are usually found giving to others in some way. They want to help. Often, they can feel taken for granted and unappreciated for what they do.

If you are a parent to a Type 2 child, it may help to draw attention to their efforts toward others, while teaching boundaries and limitations as good qualities as well. They are served by knowing that their efforts may not be appreciated by everyone. When they're not appreciated, this could easily turn into a blown-up rejection event in their minds. They can be coached to see that everyone plays their part, and it's not up to only one type to do it all. They can be taught to let that go, realizing they have much to offer.

A Type 2 recently told me, "I wish my parents would've said, 'Good job! I'm proud of you.' More often." Another Type 2 said, "My parents did not do exploring of my interior world; my thoughts and feelings . . . I think 2s can sometimes live with a feeling of not being known and, therefore, question their own stand-alone personal worth and value. Value is often felt through meeting others' needs."

A Type 3 personality wants approval. They camouflage their true feelings to meld with whoever is in the room. They can hide or deceive to be liked. Mostly, they *are* liked. But who can truly know them? Who is safe enough?

Adoptive parents of a 3 might struggle to set a table of acceptance if the house rules are rigid or expectations are high. Because they are celebrated for what they *do*, the Type 3 child often believes that they are loved and accepted only for their accomplishments. It's easy to see how an adopted Type 3 child might find it difficult to disclose their true feelings, fearing they may be discounted if they are not performing to everyone's liking. It may help the adoptive parent to know the child with a 3 descriptor is dealing with these thoughts. Perhaps the parent might look for ordinary moments throughout the week to affirm the child for just being themselves, not only connecting affirmation to what the child does.

A Type 3 recently told me, "I wish I would've heard my parents say that my failures in life don't change how they see me; that it's okay to make mistakes, even big mistakes, and no matter what I do with my life that they are still proud of me."

A Type 4 personality has deep feelings, which they long to have someone know. They sometimes share too much with the wrong person and then feel more alone than before they shared. This can be confusing when making friends. When they make friends, they struggle to keep them. There's a certain amount of abandonment they feel, which causes them to withdraw and makes it harder to maintain the relationships they have. Think of the adoptee who is a Type 4. Abandonment is already something they deal with as a result of being placed for adoption. I have, in my memory, a picture of a doorknob covered in a thorny, succulent cactus. The words underneath the picture are: "Come in." Self-sabotage is often present in relationships because they imagine others not liking them and act accordingly, which produces the result they're imagining. Fours value authenticity and will probably not get too close to others they feel aren't authentic. They love to engage on a deeper level with people, dislike small talk, and want to be understood.

How might a parent draw them out? It is important for a parent of a Type 4 to stay cool during their 4's moodiness. This might take discipline but helps the 4 navigate their moods. The parent would do well to give space to let them process their feelings. A parent could listen to their Type 4 child and affirm them for who they are because they rarely feel good enough. Acknowledging their feelings, despite the reasons for them, is helpful to the Type 4 because they want to be understood and heard.

A Type 4 recently told me, "I wish my parents would've said to me, 'You belong here. You have value. We appreciate all you offer and who you are is more important than what you do.'"

A Type 5 personality wants to be competent and insightful. They need a lot of time to reflect, and they tend to be introverted. They love copious amounts of personal space and privacy. They are bothered by what they perceive as too much "together" time with family and friends because they have a small quotient of energy they can spend like that. When they engage in a conversation, it costs them more than other numbers because of their limited bandwidth for exchange. How might feelings be hurt if others don't understand this about a 5? What could be learned and expressed by the parent if they understood this basic need of their child?

A parent might draw attention to the courage it takes to show up as the Type 5 child. Fives need to be encouraged to get things done because they are prone to live in the thinking and feeling realm most of the time. With a lot of lead time, projecting deadlines can help the 5 move from thinking and feeling in the direction of doing. How might parents be able to draw out the best while respecting and even protecting the child's need for quiet?

One 5 recently told me, "I wish my parents would have told me to cultivate my curiosity and learn how to leverage it for the benefit of myself and others. Do your research and due diligence, but then act, move forward, and take risks."

A Type 6 personality is very loyal. They are found doing whatever is best for the whole of an organization or family or entity. Though they very much want to feel certain and secure, they often jump to all the possibilities that could go wrong and feel the need to warn others because they genuinely care. Sixes find risk difficult because of their need to feel safe. Fear is a part of their internal makeup because risk is a part of life.

A parent can help their Type 6 child by telling them the truth. Because 6s find it difficult to trust, it is imperative that parents remain trustworthy. A parent can offer a listening ear to their concerns and resist saying things like, "Quit worrying about everything." As a parent gives a lot of assurances to their Type 6 child, the child feels heard and valued. It could help to encourage their child to take measured risks. Kindness is helpful when answering all their many questions. Realizing the 6's need for certainty may help the parent be more patient.

A Type 6 recently told me, "When I was young, I would've loved to have heard my parents say more about who I was versus the things I did. I do wish they would've spoken more about the gifting and talents the Lord gave me in order to steer me more in life."

Another Type 6 told me, "I wish I would've heard more words of encouragement or what I was doing right."

Type 7s do not want to miss out on anything. The routines that others enjoy make 7s bored. Type 7s are delightful people and prove to be popular because of the way they make people feel. Generally, positivity surrounds them.

Sevens possess a large need to play. A parent of a Type 7 child would do well to accept offers from their child to engage in play. And when discipline or criticism is needed, use a light-handed approach. Sometimes, inserting humor goes a long way to help them swallow the truth while being corrected.

One 7 friend of mine told me, "I wish my parents would have helped me explore more options and inspired me that life will be an adventure."

A Type 8 personality has a huge need to be in charge. They are very comfortable with confrontation and don't mind being front and center in bringing one to the room. How might a parent give this one room to explore, grow, and mature while affirming them? That's right. We all need to be affirmed *and* presented with various ways of doing things. Remember, we all have both negative and positive traits wrapped up inside. Kindness goes a long way in creating safe paths for growth. And sometimes, there will be fireworks anyway.

A parent of a Type 8 might guide them to realize that they cannot always be in charge, that others have great ideas, too, and that they could be wrong. If a parent is noticing bullying behavior, they might consider teaching listening skills to their Type 8 child and getting feedback by asking, "What did you hear?" As children, 8s need to know that they can rely on parents to care for them; that they don't have to assume full responsibility for themselves.

A Type 8 recently told me, "I wish my parents would've asked me a lot of questions and given me a chance to express my feelings. It would've created a safe place for further conversations and my understanding of the world around me."

You may have noticed that many of the Enneagram numbers wished they'd been affirmed more often by their parents. It seems universal. We all need affirmation. We all desire to be seen, heard, and understood by our parents. The difference between the numbers is their motivation behind it.

Now, you might be thinking, "How in the world am I supposed to do all this while raising other children, working, engaging in church and civic activities, and all that comes with educating them?" The short answer is: *It's what we do most of the time that matters most.* Of course, none of us are going to get it right every time. This book, in part, is for education and bringing awareness. It's helping you think and providing you with some resources, tools, and ideas to guide you on this journey of parenting the child you adopted. Along with this, I sincerely hope that you will get to the end of the book with more hope and less isolation than when you began.

Chapter Twelve

A PEEK INTO THE ADOPTED SOUL

Over the months, I've been privileged to interview several adult adoptees. Through various contacts, I've been able to connect with different individuals across the country. Their ages have spanned from twenty to seventy-two, although I did not include every interview I conducted. Though each story is unique, a theme emerged. See if you can find it.

Katy, now in her twenties, was adopted from China just before she aged out of the foster care system. She had been raised much of that time by an elderly woman. When the woman grew too old to care for her, Katy was placed in an orphanage where she lived another two and a half years before being adopted by a couple from the United States. This is her story.

The orphanage was a dark and hopeless place. The older kids would abuse the younger ones. And the nannies would too. One day, some people came to me in the orphanage, saying there was a couple in America who wanted to adopt me and asked if I'd like that. I wanted to be adopted, but I was afraid. My English wasn't good, and I feared they wouldn't understand me, and I wouldn't be able to know what they were saying to me. I was also afraid they wouldn't like me. I had already been temporarily placed in a couple's home in China, and that didn't work out at all. They sent me back to the orphanage. What if that happened again? I'd be in America all alone. As the two-and-a-half-year process unfolded, I watched, as some of my girlfriends in the orphanage were adopted by couples in Spain and America. We were all excited but very nervous for what would happen to us.

The day arrived when my adoptive parents came to meet me and pick me up. I didn't know them at all, and my English wasn't so good. Fortunately, they had with them another Chinese daughter they'd also adopted. She helped me with a little English and talked with me in my language. This helped a lot. It took about a year to really feel safe in my new home.

My parents were always nice to me, but I still felt nervous. We went to a Chinese church service each week, and there was an interpreter. We used this person to help us communicate. I also went to a language school to learn English, and that really helped me feel better.

I came to see that my parents truly cared about me. They showed me by listening to me, playing with me, and cooking food I liked. They made time for us to hang out and asked me what I was feeling and thinking while sitting with me. They tried to help me do what I wanted to do and have gotten me through the hard times.

There was a time I wanted to go back to China. I wanted to find my birth mother and wondered why she abandoned me. The elderly lady told me she found me and kept me to raise me. I always felt like I'm not good enough but didn't want to hurt my parents by talking about it. But now, I don't want to return to China. I have a family that loves me. My life has totally changed. I never knew I'd have a family, get to go to college, and have a bright future. And now I have all of that.

Sometimes, I still feel those feelings from earlier in life. Even now. Those thoughts come to me—that I was rejected and abandoned. I tell myself, "You're doing a good job. You can't listen to those lies." And I pray. One story I think of a lot is the story of Joseph in the Bible. He was sold by his brothers into slavery. He was falsely imprisoned for years. He had a long, hard journey, but he eventually ended up in a place of authority and used his influence to free his family from a famine. This gives me hope. My story can be used for the good of others.

———

Adam, in his seventies, tells his story.

I was adopted at birth. My adoptive parents had lost a biological child two years before I came along. I was their "firstborn" child. Two years later, they would adopt another baby boy, and my brother and I grew up happily together.

My parents were the best. My dad was a World War II hero, where he earned a silver star and a purple heart. My mom stayed in leadership of the Girl Scouts for seventy years. They both were very giving toward others. My dad played ball with me and had a laugh that was contagious. My mom baked around the holidays, and we would all take these baked goods to families who were less fortunate. It was a wonderful childhood where I learned manners and that it is more blessed to give than to receive.

My parents took in around twenty-five foster-care babies over time, as respite caretakers. Our family attended church regularly and prayed before dinner together.

We visited my extended family in another state often enough that I felt close to my aunts and cousins. My grandfather had been in law enforcement, and we grew up with a clear sense of right and wrong. I always felt safe with all of them and with my parents.

There were obvious differences between me and my family members. My parents were of Scandinavian descent, while I was dark-skinned with dark eyes and hair. My brother quickly grew taller than me and had light hair. Despite our physical differences, I always felt like just a normal part of the family. I was a "Jensen." They would reinforce that I was chosen, picked, and wanted all along the way while I was growing up. I remember my mom telling me it would be okay with her if I ever wanted to pursue [finding] my birth family. I really didn't want to since I had a great thing going at home. I never felt the need.

That said, when I was in my twenties and began filling out applications for this and that, I was confronted by questions of heritage, ethnicity, and so on. Also, others began asking me questions about it. I had no idea, of course. I thought briefly about trying to find out about my biological family, but I refrained because I thought it would hurt my mom.

My mom and dad passed years ago now. Their memory is such a sweet one for me. Out of curiosity, about three years ago, I submitted my DNA to ancestry.com to see what I could find out. I got a response from my biological brother, [who is] two years older than me. It was wonderful to connect. He shared a few facts, which were interesting. I learned I had eight siblings from my biological mother! They were all raised a couple of hours away. I decided [I wanted] to meet them all, and they were willing. It was really something to see physical likenesses and discover we had similar likes.

I learned I was the only child to be placed for adoption. I wondered if my biological father was an affair—like with the milkman—or a rapist. I may never know. That was really something to find out. One sibling became suspicious of my intentions of reaching out to them and renounced that I was really part of them; that there is nothing to DNA testing. This caused most of the siblings to back away. There were two that continued a relationship with me, and we're close to this day. But I felt the sting of rejection this second time, and it really hurt. Still does.

I found out my birth mother passed away about twenty-five years ago, so there's no way I can find out anything more. I now wish I could ask her things to clarify the truth. I never really wanted a relationship with her because I already had a great mother. I just wanted some answers to questions—to have my curiosity resolved.

I've decided I'm going to concentrate on the positives of what I was given by God. I had a great upbringing, a great set of loving parents, and a great life, really. I love my wife and children and feel so grateful to God for placing me in the best possible place in which to thrive. I've thought about if I had been raised by my biological mom, I would've lacked the education I have as well as many other things. I strive to live each day to the fullest. One of the best compliments I've ever received is, "I can see your dad alive in you," and that feels really good.

Rebecca, now in her thirties, relays her adoption story.

I always knew. My parents told me I grew in someone else's tummy, and they showed me children's books about adoption. My parents were always very good about being open. I remember going to pick up my baby sister when I was four years old and understood adoption pretty well. I could always ask my parents anything, felt the conversation lines were open. I also know my biological mom and grandma. I always felt I belonged. As I grew, I felt like my placement had a purpose. I mean, of all the people I could've been placed with, and I got these great parents.

Robin: *What do you wish would've been addressed but wasn't?*

Rebecca: *My adoptive mom was so selfless. I wish she would've been more open about the way she really felt . . . her own pain. I understand, as a child, she couldn't share on that level with me. But, as an adult, I wish she would've been more able to show her own pain. I'm thinking about my wedding. I felt it would be a nice gesture to invite my biological mom. I found out later that this really hurt my mom. I was just trying to be sensitive and wasn't trying to elevate her to "mother status.*

Robin: *What did you withhold as a child?*

Rebecca: *Nothing, really. I expressed everything I felt because there was freedom to do so because I knew my biological mom and grandma; I knew I was having a better life than I would be had I not been adopted.*

Robin: *Do you relate to your adoptive dad differently than your adoptive mom?*

Rebecca: *I love both of my parents, but I would say I talk with my mom almost every day, despite now living in a different state. My dad doesn't talk much, but I go to him for different things I need. I FaceTime my parents on the weekend when they're together. I love spending time with them.*

Robin: *What are your feelings about your grandparents?*

Rebecca: *My adoptive grandfather cherished me. I spent a lot of time with him, and we were very close. The out-of-state grandparents—I wasn't as close to. I think it has to do with geographic location, as well as a lack of emotional warmth, not adoption. My biological grand-mother was always careful to send me and my siblings gifts along the way. I loved her. And I'm close to my bio-logical half-siblings as well. The only thing I would say here is that once you open the door, you can't close it. There is an expectation to be more or get with them more or have more of a relationship than sometimes I want to have. It's like a stepparent, maybe.*

Robin: *What are some positives about adoption?*

Rebecca: *It helped to know from the beginning. I had a friend who was adopted that did not have the same sit-uation of knowing, and she had a difficult time. I never did. There were no surprises. I also had a great group* *of kids I grew up with who were adopted. My parents connected with other adoptive parents and children from the agency they used, as well as adoptees at our school. We adoptees had each other to compare stories, and it all just seemed so natural. I feel I accept my adoption 100 percent.*

Robin: *What are some recurring themes in your life?*

Rebecca: *I've met a lot of women who can't have children, and they ask me about adoption. Belonging is so strong for me. I always felt that if I couldn't have children, I wouldn't hesitate to adopt. I always have had purpose because of my own placement and how it came together. My parents love each other and are stable.*

Robin: *What would you like to tell the reader?*

Rebecca: *To parents, I would like to say, the more open you are, the less room there is for questions or confusion or feelings of not belonging. To adoptees, I would like to say, it's nice to find people who are going through the same as you are. There are a lot of people out there. Be sensitive to the fact that not everybody's story is the same. Find someone you can relate to.*

Deborah, in her sixties now, tells her story.

I was placed at birth into a loving home. I always knew I was adopted. There was never an announcement or surprise. I knew I was special. They told me they picked me out; they yearned for me. I always felt loved, and adoption didn't seem to affect me. I had what I thought was a normal life . . . a good childhood. I accepted it fully. I always felt safe in my home. I had a good relationship with both my parents as well as my grandparents. We lived near my dad's parents and often found ourselves in their home, playing games and enjoying our time together. I was closer to my mom's parents, who lived several states away. I guess they were warmer personalities, and we just loved them—my sister and me.

There came a time in my forties when I wondered about my medical history, and I wanted to know more about where I came from. I wanted to ask questions about menopause and other things.

I began searching online to see if I could find out anything about my birth mom. Ours was a closed adoption, and there was little information. I found a search engine about adoptees looking for their birth parents. To my surprise, I found my birth mom quickly. Her sister, unbeknownst to her, had put information on the site in case I ever reached out.

I was cautious with moving forward to meet her because I didn't want to hurt my mom. I didn't know how she'd respond. I remember talking to her, explaining that I wanted to know my medical history and was curious about my origins. I told her I'd reached out online to find my birth mom and had found her. It was a process with my mom until she came to peace about the whole thing. Once we came to an understanding, I decided to meet my birth mom.

For the first time in my life, I realized I had a missing piece I never knew existed before. Everything came together. It was the puzzle piece I didn't know I needed. There had been in me a need to belong, and I finally did belong! Knowing her history, I felt so accepted and loved. She told me her story and the events which lead up to her placing me for adoption. I loved her. She told me my biological father's name, but I promptly forgot and have not felt the need to seek him out.

This whole thing took time for my mom to fully accept. I think she felt somewhat threatened in the beginning. I was very careful with my mom because I loved her. But there was a time when we all (my adoptive parents, me, and my birth mom) met. The parents both thanked each other for the gift of me. It was quite something. Surreal.

I love the idea of adoption. There are so many kids who need loving homes to grow up in. I wish it weren't so expensive. I feel so special because I have had two sets of parents who love me.

Each time I gave birth, I wondered who they looked like. What biological resemblance is there? What traits are like my biological family?

I think what my parents did to ensure that I never felt rejection was they told me I was special. They celebrated my birthday but didn't feel the need to rehearse how I came into their lives over and over. It was normalized that I was their child. They didn't make a big deal about the fact that I was adopted. They just made me feel loved and celebrated me.

I think the adoptive parents should let the child lead with questions. When they're ready to talk about it, and they feel like it's a safe environment to ask, they will. I would like to tell adoptive parents to not stress over the fact that their children were adopted. Don't keep it a secret, but also, don't rehearse their story over and over. I think not making adoption a big, different thing is healthier for the child to feel like they're just part of the family.

―――――――――

Haley, now in her thirties, had this to say.

My earliest memory of life was when I was around five or six years old. I lived in a nice home with my biological mom and dad and my sister. My parents both had good jobs and made a good living. Our lives were relatively good except for the minimal abuse I received from my mom. I learned from an early age that I needed to protect my sister. My life was okay until my father died. That's when all he** broke loose.

I didn't understand that my mom suffered from mental illness. But I knew my world was upside down. Suddenly, with my dad being gone, there was no protector in the house, and my mom was free to do whatever she wanted. My mom abused me physically and emotionally and certainly neglected me. Sometimes, there was little to no food in the house, or we weren't allowed to touch [what was there]. I remember my sister and I eating raw potatoes together. This kind of life went on for two years. I parented my sister and told her to hide when I was being hit.

When we were put into foster care, I was twelve, and my sister was six. The day we got taken away was very traumatic for us.

After several attempts to be[reunited] with my mother over the next two to three years, the abuse continued, and at one point, my sister and I were separated and put in different foster care homes. I met my adoptive family when I was fifteen. They were fostering to adopt.

I remember feeling safe, not necessarily loved. There was plenty of food, and I was not neglected. I was excited to be in a family again, to belong. I wanted my picture to be put on their wall like any other parents would do. By their admission, they only [fostered] teenagers because nobody wanted teenagers, so they were the hardest to place. I came to see that they were looked up to and admired by their church friends for doing such a thing. It was kind of like a status symbol. As a traumatized teen-

ager in their home, they introduced me as their "adopted daughter." That really hurt and made me feel inherently broken, like nobody wanted me, like the worst goods.

I always felt like their love was conditional—if I did and said what they wanted me to do and say, if it made them look good. I tried to fit in by going to church with them and obeying the rules. Looking back, I feel I was bullied into believing in exchange for acceptance. I even tried to tan my very light-colored skin so I could look more like them. I hated my light-colored eyes because they made me look different from my family. I now see I did things I never should've had to do just to fit in.

When I got pregnant at age seventeen, I was shamed and got kicked out of their home six months after my adoption. I had brought shame to their house and reputation.

I'd been in and out of counseling for years but was also being abused during that time. Nobody would believe me because I was a child. I returned to counseling as an adult. I feel I was being helped so much until I had to quit going because of finances and time.

Now, as a parent of children, I seek to do better than what was done to me. I want to deal with my own stuff so I can be a better parent. I am more mindful of criticism about myself. On my best days, I tell myself that I can't change what happened. I remind myself to appreciate my body and that I grew two beautiful children inside my womb. On my best days, I embrace and thank my body for what it has done for me.

If I could talk to my adoptive parents right now, I would tell them to not take it personally when their child wants to look up their biological family. I wish my adoptive family would've been able to talk about it. I would also like to say, "Don't take on the Savior complex. It then becomes about you instead of providing a loving home for the child." We all want unconditional love. Be honest. Own whatever brought you to adopt this child. Trust is such an important thing.

Currently, I don't go to church anywhere. I'd say my faith lies in a universal higher energy. My adoptive parents and I aren't speaking.

———

Charli, in her twenties, shares her experience.

I was adopted at birth and honestly can't remember a single moment of finding out. I just always knew. Knowing I was adopted was a way I used to reconcile the differences between my adopted sister, mom and dad, and myself. When there were moments of not understanding each other, I would just say to myself, "Well, I'm adopted, so I guess we just don't share that sixth sense. There's bound to be a misunderstanding." At the end of the day, we loved each other and would have to work a little harder to get to that understanding.

Thinking back, I would've liked to have been asked more questions while growing up. I was and am a more private person and keep my thoughts largely to myself. But I also need someone to push a little and draw me out in order to express myself more. I also think I could've benefitted from some therapy to deal with what I felt were confusing or conflicting thoughts and emotions. I wasn't sure how to deal with them or where they were coming from. Getting counseling is considered more commonplace today than when I was growing up, but I wish I could've talked with someone to help me process through this earlier in life.

I always felt I had to live up to labels: happy, dancer, pianist, good student, and extroverted. If I ever expressed anything other than what was expected, I felt like there was something wrong with me and that I was not supposed to be feeling any other way. I was introduced to people being these things because they were proud of me. But I guess I felt like that was what defined me.

I wish I would've had the space in our home to express my thoughts freely. I refrained because I felt my thoughts might be too different from the family and from what I was taught. I did always feel loved, just a bit hampered by free expression. Looking back, I wish my parents would've opened a door for me to explore and express emotions. I didn't feel free to talk openly about sex, drinking, drugs, political opinions, and more. I felt they were somehow so perfect they wouldn't understand all that I was dealing with and hearing at school. I knew the "right" talk I'd learned at home and church and didn't feel like I could bring up things I was thinking about or wondering. I always felt such a huge shame because "good" Christians did not think or question anything. I would've loved for my parents to tell me about their struggles while growing up or things they went through that were hard. I learn from stories; they create an atmosphere of honesty and openness without the shame associated with life.

Regarding my birth mother, I always felt I'd like to meet her someday. I felt the freedom from my parents to do so, that it wouldn't hurt them. I've also never felt pressured to meet her. At this point in my life, I feel it'd be too much for me. I want stability in my life before meeting her. I'm afraid it would add chaos to my life that I couldn't handle. I have existing relationships I'd like to cultivate rather than delve into a new one where I'm pretty sure she'd want more out of it than I could give at this point in my life. I wish that, while growing up, I would've been able to know more about her story and what led up to my being placed.

When it comes to my biological dad, I guess I've never had much respect for him, but I also don't know what really happened. I choose to not hold it against him. I think I've been most curious about medical history, heritage, personality traits, and things like that.

I love my grandparents, although we lived far away, geographically, to both sets. I loved hearing their stories, and it helped me understand my parents better. But when

I was with my cousins, I sometimes felt sad because I didn't have that DNA thing that connected me with my grandparents like they did. Grandparents represent roots in a way that the family tree then stems.

I'd like to say here that I've seen some recurring themes in my life. I definitely have a heightened sensitivity to rejection, especially with personal relationships with family and significant others. I have always found that I needed a lot more affirmation from teachers and teacher figures. I've always been a performer and overly critical of myself when I don't perform as well as I know I can. Being a perfectionist, I almost never reach that level though, so it took me a long time to accept that I was not how well I did on a certain day.

I also realize I have a heightened sense of shame. Very often, it's my first instinct to take negative things as shame and not being good enough. The mix of being a perfectionist, a performer, and never really feeling good enough has made me work very hard. I always want to better myself. I think I'm dealing with it now in a healthier way than I did when I was younger.

I have noticed that it's easy for me to make new friends and move on from people groups and friends, depending on where I live. It's been much rarer to keep friends.

I think adoption has provided me with a fun conversation starter. My favorite thing is when people say how alike my family members and I all look, and I think we've grown to look more alike over the years. I think it's super cool when people are surprised that I was adopted, and it makes me proud to say, "Yeah, it is amazing how God put our family together. We were handpicked, and we are all what each of the other needs and did not know at the time."

When I was young, I would fantasize about my genetic heritage and let my imagination run wild. Then, in my early twenties, I did genetic testing and found it fascinating to discover my biological heritage. It was neat how I already identified with a lot of the results, even before knowing them.

Another thing I love about being adopted is I think it's helped me to connect with different people with similar experiences. It's that moment of having that unspoken understanding and camaraderie.

———————

Craig, now in his sixties, relays his story.

I was adopted at birth and found out when I was very young. I always felt special, loved, supported, and all my needs were met. I didn't ever think about meeting my birth parents because I loved my family and felt very much a part of them. I had no holes, really.

My mom told me she'd help me find my birth mom if I ever wanted to. There were no secrets in our home about adoption. I always felt free to ask, and they answered what they could with the information they had.

The story of my birth mother was that she was passing through town and delivered me at the local hospital. It turns out that a certain nurse at the time helped deliver me. My birth mom told the hospital she didn't want the baby (me) and that nurse adopted me and became my mother. I knew nothing else. My parents had a biological daughter, and she was my sister, and we were relationally close.

I always felt loved in that I was provided with nice clothes and a college education, and they taught me well about the world I lived in. They were fair and encouraging to me. We all went to church regularly, and I was a beneficiary of an encouraging church family. My faith has impacted my life greatly. My decisions have been aligned with the Christian faith, and my parents gave me that. I'm so grateful.

I never really wanted to look up anything about my biological father or mother. Because I had some physical struggles in later years, my own daughters were more interested in me finding out more about my birth family than I was. I think it was medical history-related. To satisfy their curiosity, I submitted DNA to ancestry.com. I found a biological sister who had retired from the same career I'd retired from. Her situation was the same as mine; as in, our birth mom walked into a hospital in another state and delivered her and placed her for adoption.

I will never understand how my birth mom could do what she did. There's much I don't know about her situation. I wish I could know more about why she did what she did. I would like to tell all birth mothers to please consider giving your child a better chance if you can't take care of them. No telling where I would've ended up if I'd been raised by someone who didn't want me. I've thanked God many times for being placed in the home I was placed in. I'd say adoption is something everyone ought to consider if they can't conceive a child on their own. I'm a firm believer in adoption.

———

Chloe, in her twenties, shares her ups and downs.

I was born in China and lived in two different orphanages before I was adopted and brought to the USA. My life in the orphanages was sad and lonely. I think I always wanted to be loved and understood by someone special but didn't have a concept of a family, per se. I had friends at the orphanage, but not what I'd call loving friends, necessarily. We were just kids who played together.

I was introduced to the concept of adoption at around five years old, and it took two years for the adoption to be completed. My adoptive family would send pictures and gifts during that time, and I began to understand more about what adoption meant. I was afraid of them because my mom had curly, flaming red hair. Also, in the family's picture, they all had red eyes (because of the flash of the camera), and I thought they were aliens. Even with this picture, I hoped they could love and understand me for who I was.

It has taken a lifetime for me to understand their love. At first, I tried to be the perfect child. I didn't know English, and I was completely dependent on them for survival. I knew they had paid a lot of money for my adoption, and I didn't want to disappoint them. I also had a fear I could be sent back to the orphanage if I proved to be a problem. I wanted to please them. I felt as though I had to earn my keep. This feeling has accompanied me throughout my entire growing up. But there came a point when I was done pleasing.

I acted out in various ways and was afraid of my own emotions, not fully able to express how I was feeling. I remember stuffing it all and having big outbursts about once a year. Triggers for me were the feeling of being rejected or the feeling of being a failure.

I got counseling, and it was good. But I'd say the hurting child needs a lot more. I needed someone to walk beside me through the counseling. I needed "pillars" to talk with when those feelings came up from the counseling. I talked with my parents, my parent's friends, and my sister.

I loved that when I was upset and crying, my parents would say things like, "You can cry for your birth parents and the friends you left behind." This gave me the freedom to grieve that I don't look like my parents. I think I overcame some of the feelings of "less than" when I real-ized I don't have to compete for my value. My mom and dad were so intentional about showing me my value. They would see in me something and validate it. They might say something like, "Wow, that's what makes you, you. You are so valuable."

My parents were great at being open with me about adoption. Because we looked so different, it was always there. I liked that they didn't shy away from my ethnic-ity, but I wish they would've let me choose how much I wanted to identify with it without feeling like it was being pushed on me. Sometimes, it magnified that I was different when I just wanted to feel part of the family. I wanted to fit in. So, I'd say it was good to be open about it but not always focused on it.

I think a real understanding of what I had been given finally came to me while recovering from a suicide attempt at age twenty-three. My sister brought me a Styrofoam cup with the written words YOUR FAMILY LOVES YOU on it. My mind took me back to the orphanage years ago when I wanted unconditional love and understanding from someone. I realized then that I'd been given just that through this family. They had shown this to me for all these years. I could finally accept it.

I'd like to tell other adoptees that life gets better. I'd like to tell them to talk about their feelings . . . not just the rage, but all of their feelings. Talk about when you have that feeling that you don't belong. Express it to parents or siblings. Don't isolate. When we try to figure it out alone, we just spiral down. I learned that they're not going to get rid of me, no matter what.

I'd like to tell parents that, when adopting, they should consider birth order. My choice would be to adopt first or at least in the middle of biological kids. When you're the last one, it's easy to feel you are an afterthought or that someone felt they needed to rescue you. It was easy to think that instead of believing these people really wanted me. I would've liked to have been the one to babysit or help with the others to feel like a contributor or an integral part of the family.

One last thing I'd like to say to parents: while growing up, celebrating "Gotcha Days" or "Adoption Days" or even sometimes birthdays were a reminder of the trauma of my past. When my story was told to me year after year, it didn't feel like a good thing. It was a reminder of how I was different and didn't fit.

———

Richard, in his fifties, was adopted at birth. He has two younger siblings—one adopted and one biological. Here is his story.

My earliest recollection of being adopted was one of acceptance and normalcy. My parents were open all along about the subject. My grandparents were loving and supportive. I wasn't very curious about my family of origin early on. I had so many interests in school, and I was busy. I suppose I wondered, on occasion, about my birth parents but put it out of my mind quickly. I think knowing my parents told me I was welcome to look her up when I reached the age of twenty-one gave me just enough info to put it on the back burner. I was largely unaffected by this fact for most of my growing-up years.

There were times when people would talk about their heritage that I didn't have much to say. I wondered about mine. Sometimes, I even fantasized about my father being a character out of a movie or something. I had a vivid imagination. However, this didn't consume my thoughts. I just didn't dwell on it.

My adoptive parents were and are my parents. They were great. My dad was interested in character-building programs for youth, and I became interested in the same things. My mom had a passionate fire for certain things, and I feel I've taken that on in different ways throughout my life too. I would say she taught me to have devotion to family, which has served me to this day.

Both of my parents were very supportive in that they would attend my many concerts, plays, games, and other activities while growing up. I was more extroverted in the things I enjoyed doing, and they were more introverted. We didn't look the same, and our personalities were most definitely different. Despite this fact, they were my parents, and I loved them.

It wasn't until my forties that I became curious enough to look up my birth mom. I think this was brought on by my marriage and then thinking about having our own children. In considering this, I thought I might be met with a hostile or shunning response. [Or, I knew] I could also be well-received. I just didn't know what I'd find. Curiosity grew within me until I decided to find her. One winter night, I sat down in my comfortable chair and dialed the number. I had no idea what I was going to say. I just did it.

A kind voice answered the phone and out tumbled the words: "Hi. I'm Richard. You don't know me, but does the date February 12, 1968 (real date changed to protect identity) mean anything to you?" She haltingly said, "Yes. It does." After a few more words, she confirmed she was my birth mother.

It turns out she was so relieved to hear from me. She was happy I was doing so well in life. She'd felt guilty for her decision those forty-some years ago, even though she felt it was the best thing she could do for me. I was able to affirm her decision and thank her. It was very special to help relieve some of this burden that she'd carried all those years.

I've been a little more reserved when it comes to reaching out to my birth father. I think I'm not sure I have the bandwidth to maintain a relationship with more than my birth mom right now. I have been able to meet my half-sister, who has been a joy to know. I will say a lot of connecting the dots has happened for me since I met my birth mom. She and I share the same sense of humor, and we are both more extroverted. I found a picture of my birth father "back in the day," and I'm almost an exact replica of him when he was this age. It filled in some holes for me. It helped me know more about who I am. Since then, discovering my ethnicity and culture has encouraged me and helped me make more sense of why I am the way I am.

My birth mother, for instance, shares my strong work ethic, strive for excellence, and organizational skills. I am a recovering perfectionist—ha! We're both efficient. It's settling to know these things.

The surprising thing for me has been my parents' reaction to me finding my birth mom. It was shocking to hear that they didn't want to know anything about her or my interactions with her. It felt like I'd been bushwhacked. I would've loved for them to say something like, "Hey, what was that like for you?" or "How did that make you feel?" Instead, I was met with such resistance that it has put a distance between us since that day. I'm really sad about this and wish they wouldn't be hurt by it and that we could have open discussions. I wish I could get back to an authentic relationship with them again and that they could understand I love them while also needing to meet my birth mom.

I can appreciate the skills and opportunities that nurture gave me through my adoptive parents and the inner leanings and personality I gained through nature via my birth parents.

————————

Carina, in her thirties, shares her story.

I suppose my earliest recollection of being adopted is when I asked my mom for a baby, thinking we were going to go to a store and pick up a sister or brother. I thought we'd just go and pick out the one we wanted and take them home. So, in a way, early in life, I felt "picked" or chosen. Of course, as I grew older, I realized adoption doesn't quite work that way, but I still felt special because of the way my parents told my story. It always sounded a bit like a fairytale. ("We couldn't have children, and then we found you.")

I think knowing I was adopted changed over time. When I was a child, I was confident in my adoption. I thought I was even cooler than the other kids because I had been chosen. It really wasn't until I got older that it affected me differently. The first negative response to my adoption story that I can remember was when I was thirteen. This guy said, "Oh, I'm so sorry!" [upon learning I was adopted], and I felt the need to assure him it was a good thing—that I was happy with my adoptive parents and how things ended up. Though, it made me reluctant to share it so freely again. It wasn't because I felt an internal struggle but because it made me feel like being adopted was something that would be misunder-

stood by others, as if I were an unfortunate or unwanted child instead of it being a thoughtful, loving decision made in my best interest.

Of course, that was my perspective as a child. I had no clue until the last five years that I had deep-seated issues that were related to my origin story. It was buried under this happy-go-lucky story I had heard and told for many years. Even I didn't know that I had an emotional history because I went home with my adoptive parents as an infant, so when I had deep-seated, internal pain, I didn't know what to point to. I figured I had a peachy life—a life that anyone would envy. For the most part, we were a well-off, peaceful family who went out of their way to celebrate each other's birthdays and holidays. I felt guilty and ungrateful for being in pain, like something was wrong with me, as I got older.

I always knew I was adopted, so I didn't really have questions, per se. As I grew, more details surrounding my birth came out, and I felt like my parents handled the divulging of those details in an age-appropriate way. When I got significantly older, I wanted to know more about my birth father. Mainly, I was always curious about his cultural background because I knew he came from a South American country. I blended in pretty well with my adoptive family since my skin color was close to theirs, despite the Hispanic ethnicity of my birth father. I often passed as my parents' [biological] child, but anyone who looked closely asked about my heritage. Probably because of that prompting, I often felt like there was an entire history and cultural identity that I was missing out on or couldn't access. Unfortunately, all the questions I had were questions neither my adoptive parents nor my birth mother would have been able to answer. My birth mom didn't know him or where to locate him.

At some point in my growing-up years, the feeling that adoption was special was replaced with a sense of feeling out of place, weird, or that I didn't fit. In middle school, I had my first run-in with mean girls. I realize that backstabbing and betrayal are common experiences for most preteens, but, they were deeply traumatic events for me, even though they couldn't be defined as abuse. When I got older, I felt ashamed of how little resilience I had. I now realize it was triggering an internal feeling of rejection that was already there, which made me super sensitive to the rejection and criticism of others.

Since I didn't understand it, I thought I was broken, that there was something wrong with me. When I got older and could compare my stories to others, I felt ungrateful for being in pain because I had gotten the "best end of the stick" in terms of loving parents and access to opportunities I wouldn't have had otherwise.

I always framed my adoption story as a positive because it is. But sometimes, it felt fake because there was a part of me that wondered, "Well, if my life is so wonderful, then why am I still in pain? It must be me."

Growing up, I always felt physically safe in my home, but not in very many other places for overnight visits. Unless it was with my grandparents, cousins, or godparents, I never slept well. I was, what you might call hyper-vigilant, on guard. Even when I was left alone at home, I was fearful of something bad happening to me. I had an irrational fear of "bad men" breaking in when nothing like that had ever happened. To this day, I make sure all blinds are down and doors are locked. I've noticed open blinds and unlocked doors don't bother other people like they do me.

I want to say . . . I didn't always feel emotional safety. I sometimes felt that it wouldn't be good for me to express negative emotions. There were clear standards for behavior. I was taught to express love, joy, kindness, peace, and patience. I think that's important. But I didn't know what to do with the other emotions, like anger. I was taught to not throw tantrums, but I didn't know how to deal with the anger I felt. So I learned to repress it in unhealthy ways until I exploded. I would've liked to have been invited to process anger, to talk about why I was angry, and to explore the underlying reason. I had no realization that I could've been angry about things that happened to me or my birth mother before my conception and immediately after my birth.

When I think about meeting my birth mother, I have been restrained because it might require more of me than I can give. I have been afraid it might produce conflict, not only for my parents but for me. I've been afraid it might cause confusion and even an identity crisis. I didn't want to do anything to disrupt the attachment I feel with my adoptive family. I am curious about certain things, like history, but am not looking for a close relationship. I've thought that if I opened that door, I wouldn't be able to shut it. I sometimes feel pressured by others who've heard my story to "open that door." I can feel unloving or that something is wrong with me for not wanting to open it just yet. But it's important to me that I feel ready. Even if I do decide to meet her, I will, more than likely, feel the need to set up boundaries to feel safe.

I've had curiosities about meeting my birth father but only for seeing physical similarities or learning about the culture. I would like to know more about the history of his family, but not badly enough to seek this out. I've not had much affection due to him forcing himself on my birth mother, resulting in my being conceived. I have a good understanding of why I was placed for adoption and have supported her decision. I think my anger has been directed toward him, probably. I've not gotten counseling, so maybe I would understand this dynamic better if I were to talk this out. Even with this realization, on some emotional level, I want to know that both my birth parents wanted me. I know my birth mother wanted me and couldn't care for me. I'm glad to know she wanted me. As far as my birth father? It makes no rational sense, but yes, I want to know he wants me even though I'm glad he didn't raise me, and I'm not in his life. To ask a question, you must be prepared to get the answer you may not want. I'm still not ready to ask him that question.

As a teenager, I internalized messages that said I wasn't worthy, was weird, and wasn't good enough or wanted. I wish my parents would've addressed some of those things head-on more often. It may have helped me better navigate middle school and high school, in particular.

I had a lot of inordinate rage as a child and as a teen, and I didn't understand why. Perhaps it might've been helpful to hear that some emotions I was experiencing may have their root in my birth story. Unfortunately, the way it was dealt with was to correct the behavior and not deal with the root cause. If we'd recognized it may have been rooted in abandonment or rejection, perhaps I would've learned how to deal with anger in a healthier way. I feel like I pushed it down and suppressed it in order to behave correctly. It has remained an issue well into my adulthood.

I love my adoptive parents very much. I loved hearing about the story of my birth periodically and feel it helped to reframe adoption in a positive light. It may have helped to have additional periodic reminders that they were available if I had questions from time to time, stemming from feelings of unworthiness or anger . . . to talk through and even pray through it. Negative feelings were mostly brought on by others' comments. I would've liked to know they weren't afraid of my emotions.

There was a stigma surrounding getting counseling when I was growing up. My parents offered it, but this made me feel, all the more, that there was something wrong with me. I thought things like, "I must be so bad at making and keeping friends, I have to pay a professional friend to listen to me," and "I am so broken and need to be fixed." I would've loved to have heard something from them like, "It's normal for adoptees to need counseling. There's nothing wrong with you. It might be another way to think through things if you're struggling and if there are some things you're not comfortable processing with us."

At this stage in my life, I can see some recurring themes. I have struggled a lot with feeling rejected, weird, different, or like I don't belong or fit in. Feelings of unworthiness and not being good enough have accompanied me. I was always trying to prove I was good enough, so I went above and beyond in things like character and academic achievement. I've been very performance-oriented. Although I'm a hard worker, finding my place in a career that suits me has been very difficult. That's probably related to my struggle with identity. I was very sensitive to every sign of rejection, abandonment, and betrayal, and my emotional experience intensified. For me, that was normal. I didn't realize it was intensified because I'm an adoptee. That dawned on me in my early twenties.

I have also struggled with recurring bouts of depression, rage, loneliness, anxiety, and self-hatred. I now see this began around the age of nine to ten years old.

Self-sabotage is a recurring theme in my life. I seem to sabotage my own chances at emotionally intimate rela-

tionships and having a successful life, even though I deeply desire it. I want to thrive. There's always been a ceiling, a deep internal frustration, or a feedback loop that keeps me from living at my highest potential.

Last, I'd like to say that I believe adoption is a positive thing—a redemptive thing. Knowing that I was chosen means so much to me and dispels the myth that I was Plan B. I was always Plan A. Every adoption is messy. There is still healing that needs to take place, and there's growing in that healing that helps one enjoy the "happy ending" they've been given. I believe, for the parents, it's a happy ending. I think there's a misconception that it's also a happy ending for the child. I'd say it's more like a second beginning. They already had a beginning that they will reckon with as they get older. Adoption doesn't erase it. It's not a do-over.

For example, I've realized that as I've grown up, specific issues I've struggled with my entire life are probably related to my origin story, although I didn't make that connection until my late twenties. Even though I wouldn't have wanted it to happen any other way, I still have to acknowledge and process those emotions and learn how to walk in healing. The first step for me was to recognize those emotions are normal, that I'm not ungrateful, and there's nothing wrong with me. There is an explanation for my pain, and pain needs to be witnessed and acknowledged before it can be healed. For the past few years, that's where I've been. It's not a fun place to be, but you can't skip it.

Chapter Thirteen

COMING TO PEACE INSIDE DISCOMFORT

I've thought much about what it means to be adopted. I know firsthand what it is to raise adoptees. In the research I've done, I've learned a lot about trauma and factors that affect behavior in the adoptee. It is my hope, in reading this book, you have too. It has been such a great privilege to hear directly from adoptees and birth moms and adoptive parents. Each group has its own unique set of struggles around adoption. And these struggles can and do ease with education, understanding, and the will to do better. But it is a lifelong endeavor.

Nature has always called to me in different ways. I love to hike, fish, and watch our dog run wild along the path. She runs with abandon. She runs for the sheer joy of it. She is with her favorite people doing her favorite thing, and all in her world is right.

This is what I imagined a family created by adoption would be like. Each one would be comfortable in their own skin, would be secure in each other's love, would enjoy being together, and all would be right in their world. When this vision was shattered by the "wild card hammer," it took me a long time to recover my equilibrium.

If adoption is so hard, why do it? At my worst, I felt like I had ruined these kids. I wondered why I was chosen to raise them since I'd done such a horrible job, as evidenced by the fact that the story didn't unfold as I'd imagined it would.

Recently I've been thinking about the image of a tree. I have in my mind a sturdy, established tree, not a young sapling or a new start. Think with me for a bit about what a live tree offers. I think of steadfastness. A mature tree has strong limbs with lots of leaves or fruit. It's not easily downed by storms or injury. It provides shade from the blistering sun. It can support a swing attached by ropes, giving humans a place to dream. It seems to hug children as they climb it. It gives oxygen into the air for us to breathe. Its roots go down deep into the soil, and its branches reach to the sky. It's a place of rest for birds who are weary or just need a place to hide. Sometimes, it is referred to as a landmark by which people can find their way. The tree doesn't shout out. Its beauty silently remains for all passersby. Even if people don't praise its existence, its strength would be missed if cut down. Isn't this like the family?

The family created by adoption is also like a tree. I see the same tree with all the attributes mentioned above. The difference is this tree has the added strength of limbs having been grafted in.

To graft a limb, the injured branch is strategically fitted onto a specific place on a mature tree. With roots already established, this mature tree receives the branch. In time, only the horticulturist can tell where the grafting occurred. It has simply become an integral part of the whole. It has some of its original qualities but now has also taken on the qualities of the rooted tree. Does this sound familiar? Grafting often takes place with fruit trees where a new hybrid is desired. Often, the end product is delightful. That's not to say that grafting isn't painless. If a tree could talk, it may say, "Yeah, that was a little rough in the beginning. The injury alone made me wonder if it would take."

Adoption is a lot like grafting. The adoptee has original trauma. You might call them the "injured branch." The mature tree might be likened to the family. With roots established, it receives the injured branch. Even though there is pain involved, with patience, there is growth through suffering.

Why are we humans so afraid of suffering? We all love the growth part. But if you're like me, you just want to wake up "grown" without having to go through anything difficult. I have met people who have suffered and have chosen not to grow. But I have met no one who has grown without suffering being part of the equation.

When we choose to adopt, we must see that this is for the long haul. We must realize that all those who have been adopted come with trauma. We must go into this venture with our eyes wide open. We must examine and minimize our expectations. There was a time when my expectations went from "They'll be somebody so gifted and known, they'll excel for their whole life" to "If I can just keep them alive until their brain kicks in, that'll be success."

We must be willing to learn and change. And yes, we must keep the love on. For the rest of our lives. We don't get a pass when they turn eighteen to quit loving or learning. It is for the rest of our lives.

I was reading recently about ancient Roman culture. Unbeknownst to me, adoption was common. If the owner of the estate didn't have a son who could manage the fortune or who was irresponsible or had no sons at all, this man could decide to adopt a worthy soul of his choosing. This adoptee received all the wealth, property, and goods of the adoptive parent, sparing nothing. They were fully received in every way. An interesting fact of this finding was that this same adoptive parent could disown his own biological son if deemed appropriate to do so, but the adoption was irreversible. When the choice was made to adopt, it stood. You might say that commitment to adoption, in this instance, was stronger than blood.

My husband Jon and I have talked much about adoption and have grown through the painful realizations, discoveries, and conversations we've experienced. I thought you'd like to hear his perspective on coming to peace. These are his words.

I'm certain that the adoption process has evolved over the last thirty-one years. Adoptive parents are receiving much better preparation through education, counseling, and resources—provided by their adoption agencies—that hopefully prepare them for the challenges and differences they may encounter raising an adopted child versus a biological child. However, the end goal in most adoptive parents' hearts is a sincere hope that our adoptive children will see us as Father and Mother. The adoptive parents want that close, intimate relationship, one demonstrated by childlike trust, confidence, and affection.

Most adoptive parents want their adopted children to see them as their daddy or mommy and freely express their affection for them. However, unless adoptive parents understand the challenges of trust in the hearts of their adoptive children, they are likely to become discouraged. Affection, confidence, and trust have an arch enemy within the soul of an adoptee. Its name is Fear, *and it enslaves their hearts, minds, and souls. It must be defeated to create a new pathway for the adoptee, one that genuinely expresses these attributes.*

I didn't see this challenge clearly as I raised our two daughters. I was unaware of their captivity through fear and the helpless defeat that surrounds the soul of an adoptee. I could not understand how anyone could hear from their parents every day of their life how loved they are and how wonderful they are and still be held captive to fears of rejection, inferiority, lack of belonging, and being undesirable. I failed to realize that no affirmation, no gift, no declaration of my love, no daily hug, and no understanding ear would work. They were dealing with a powerful foe from within that kept them from freely receiving us. In other words, they had a belief system that always circled back to the negative aspects of their adoption circumstances rather than embracing their adoption as the beautiful provision it was.

As adoptees grow into adults, they begin to explore their childhood beliefs and feelings about their adoption circumstances, many of which have followed them into adulthood. Although they have let go of the "Will my parents send me back?" question, there are still thoughts and fears at various levels, ones that overwhelm and paralyze their progress.

One of the most important parts of understanding the adoption process is that it's not only the adoptive parents that need to adopt the child, but it's the adoptee that needs to adopt the adoptive parents. By doing this, the adoptee embraces their circumstances and receives the gift called adoption. Just because someone hands you a gift doesn't mean it has to be opened and enjoyed. Many adoptees receive the lavishly wrapped gift and then set it aside without having explored its contents, afraid of what might be inside. A metamorphosis must take place in the heart of an adoptee instigated by their acceptance of the beautiful provision for their lives.

The fear of being rejected, not being good enough, not belonging, or not being wanted melt away in the acknowledgment that their life was not a mistake but was masterfully planned and their future secured by the providence of adoption. In other words, the adoptee must accept that their adoption was meant for their ultimate good. Will there be unanswered questions? Yes. However, those questions will no longer enslave the mind, ravage the soul, and destroy emotional stability. Rather, the lack of knowledge will surrender to the freedom of awareness that adoption was Plan A.

What does that look like for the adoptee? No longer do they ask themselves, "I wonder what was so wrong with me that I was given away?" Rather, they acknowledge the intrinsic value of themselves, their adoptive parents, and their environments and bless them instead of cursing them. They find the courage to engage with people and choose to believe good about themselves. They move away from the feeling of being a misfit and into seeing themselves as the blessings they are to their adoptive families.

Many adoptees I spoke with found peace when they met their birth family or birth mom. Some didn't know they needed to, but when they did, many loose ends came together for them. In doing this, they came to a restful peace about their lives. Others haven't wanted to meet their birth moms or family members, feeling it's all too much to manage.

You met Elizabeth earlier in Chapter Four. She was my childhood friend who was the "good kid" I was intimidated by while growing up. I recently asked her how she came to find peace about the whole adoption issue in her life. She walked me through, in more detail, how her heart was settled over time.

Elizabeth says:

> *Well, life is hard. As I've gotten older, I've been able to put myself in my birth mom's shoes. Back in the fifties, when I was born, there was little provision for someone who ended up pregnant while being unmarried. In her case, her father was a pastor of a strict denomination, and there was a lot of shame attached. If I'd been in that situation, I'm sure I might've done what she did.*
>
> *So now, I can give her a lot of slack. How hard that must have been for her. I wish I could now have a relationship with her to tell her she did a good thing for me, that I've had a wonderful life because of her courageous decision.*
>
> *I also think because I know more about grace and forgiveness and how it's changed me, I've healed and grown. I can see how much grace has been in my life, and I'm grateful for it. I've chosen to see that grace over my life instead of having a pity party.*

When my adoptive mom died, I went through another time of feeling like an orphan in the world. It caught me off-guard. I found myself having to adjust to adoption all over again. It was fresh grief. The thing that helped was I went through my family and listed every cousin and aunt who'd experienced adoption or even gone through a divorce. Some had adopted internationally, others had domestic adoptions. There were single parents, stepparents, and half-sibling groups. I thought about each of them and how they must feel. And then I didn't feel alone anymore. The world is full of people who live with these facts every day. It just helped me come to grips with the fact that I've had a good life and still do. It's just part of my story.

Coming to peace is a long and difficult journey for some. The path has detours, obstacles, and, sometimes, years of uncertainty. I suppose I could say this of all of humanity. But what I've noticed in my sixty-plus years of being on the planet is, true peace comes with a heaping helping of forgiveness along the way. Bitterness never offers that peace. When we choose to see things the way they are instead of insisting that they be like we want them to be, it opens us up for learning. We've all heard it said that education is power. I would agree, in part.

But besides love itself, I would say the power of forgiveness trumps the power of education. Forgiveness can carry us while we limp along for understanding. Forgiveness can bring clarity to a situation. When we have clarity, hope can come.

Maybe this is a good place to pause and drink deeply of forgiveness over our own lives. Maybe we need to forgive ourselves for the way we've responded to our adoptees because we didn't understand. Maybe we need to forgive their family of origin for their choices to use drugs or alcohol during pregnancy—or for abuse or neglect, thereby making it harder on our children and us. Maybe we need to forgive those who didn't understand the cards we've been dealt in raising adoptees; all the messages and judgment we and our children have endured. Some of us might even feel tricked by God. If that's you, maybe you need to forgive Him.

For those of us who feel forgiveness is "letting them off the hook," I want to say I disagree. In my experience, when I imagine myself absolving someone, it doesn't negate what they've done. Rather, it sets me free from the bitterness. I don't have to make everything right. I get to live free knowing it's not my responsibility to fix any of it. Me being bitter won't affect anyone but me. Letting it all go is a way of practicing self-compassion. It's a relief, really—the lightening of a heavy load. If you've been able to identify something inside your heart that doesn't belong, I encourage you to do what you must to be free.

Education, acknowledgment, vulnerability, and forgiveness pave the way to peace. While love is always present, it's not a stand-alone remedy with adoption. I sincerely hope that every adoptive parent can come to peace and learn to access joy. It is a beautiful undertaking to embrace a child with different DNA. It is a courageous road. The grafting of the two won't come without pain. Owning our mistakes and an understanding of the specific differences in raising the adoptee versus a biological child can help us on our way forward.

I hope this book has shed light on things you haven't known before. Perhaps you've experienced your own starry-eyed to wide-eyed circumstances. I hope you can begin giving yourself some slack in your perfectionist tendencies. It is my sincere desire to create a safe place for coming together for all of us who have felt we've been alone. May resilience be our companion. May courage be our mantra. And may our love move us closer to coming to peace.

Gratitudes

Huge thank you to my lifelong partner and best friend, Jon, for your massive support and love through thick and thin. You're still the one.

Thank you to Bev Kline and Carol Morgan, who've given their lives for the adoption triad.

Thank you to all the courageous adoptive parents, adoptees and birth moms who told their stories to help others.

Thank you to Karan, my open-eyed friend, for being willing to learn and detangle right along with me.

Thank you to Nancy for your listening ear, encouragement, and priceless feedback. You make me want to be better every day.

Thank you to Susan for helping me make connections with beautiful people and for your continued friendship.

Thank you to Cheri, my eye-opener friend. You have helped me unpack. I treasure you.

Thank you to Diane, Jo, and Beverly for being there from before I was starry-eyed and every day since.

Thank you to Tammy Lynn, for your demonstrated love throughout our adult years together and for your belief in this project and in me.

Thank you to Lynn and Kristina, for your selfless acts and entrusting us with so much.

Thank you to Mallory and Autumn for your openness and for teaching me courage, communication, and how to keep digging for the gold.

And finally, thank you to Morgan James Publishing for helping me take this resource far and wide.

About The Author

Robin Hitt, a retired registered nurse, is an author and adoptive parent. Being a credentialed life and business coach, a Certified Daring Way™ facilitator, and a lifelong learner, she loves helping adoptive parents through her writing, coaching, speaking, and media interviews. She and her husband of more than four decades reside in Colorado, where she enjoys time with her adult daughters, entertaining friends, hiking (with her doggie), fishing, and making new discoveries in nature.

To contact Robin for coaching, workshops, or speaking, email robin@robinhitt.com or call (719) 435-0777. Website is robinhitt.com

Additional Resources

For more information on these topics, visit the respective organizations' websites. Please note: This is not an exhaustive list, and the author and publisher do not certify or necessarily agree with any information on these sites. You can find more information at RobinHitt.com, where you can also ask about Robin's availability for speaking or learn about her workshop schedule.

GENERAL ADOPTION

- *Adoption Therapy: Perspectives from Clients and Clinicians on Processing and Healing post-Adoption Issues by Laura Dennis*
- *The Body Keeps the Score: Brain, Mind, and Body in the Healing of Trauma by Bessel Van Der Kolk, M.D.*
- *Being Adopted: The Lifelong Search for Self by David M. Brodzinsky, Ph.D., Marshall D. Schechter, M.D., and Robin Marantz Henig*
- *"The 20 Things Adoption" podcast by Sherrie Eldridge*
- *"Adoption Now" podcast by April Fallon*
- *A Love-Stretched Life by Juliana Goble*
- *Kay Holler (kayholler.com)*
- *Life in the Trinity Blog (lifeinthetrinity.com) *Click the homepage and scroll to the bottom for the latest podcasts.*

- *Adoptioncenter.us (to find an adoption center near you and what they offer)*
- *showhope.org (learn through conferences hosted by these folks)*

RAD
- *The Mayo Clinic (mayoclinic.org)*
- *Webmd.com*

NEUROFEEDBACK
To find a practitioner in your area, go to bcia.org and click "Find a Practitioner." You can plug in your zip code to locate a local professional.

SELF-COMPASSION
- self-compassion.org

PERSONALITY ASSESSMENTS
- Disc Assessment: discpersonalitytesting.com
- Big Five: truity.com
- Myers-Briggs: myersbriggs.org
- Enneagram of Personality: WEPPS.com, enneagraminstitute.com, or typologyinstitute.com
- Your Enneagram Coach: yourenneagramcoach.com (Jeff was adopted). You can sign up for podcasts to come to your inbox at this site.

A free ebook edition is available with the purchase of this book.

To claim your free ebook edition:

1. Visit MorganJamesBOGO.com
2. Sign your name CLEARLY in the space
3. Complete the form and submit a photo of the entire copyright page
4. You or your friend can download the ebook to your preferred device

Morgan James BOGO™

A **FREE** ebook edition is available for you or a friend with the purchase of this print book.

CLEARLY SIGN YOUR NAME ABOVE

Instructions to claim your free ebook edition:
1. Visit MorganJamesBOGO.com
2. Sign your name CLEARLY in the space above
3. Complete the form and submit a photo of this entire page
4. You or your friend can download the ebook to your preferred device

Print & Digital Together Forever.

Snap a photo

Free ebook

Read anywhere